CHURCH AHEAD

MOVING FORWARD WITH CONGREGATIONAL SPIRITUAL PRACTICES

Academy of Parish Clergy
Guides to Practical Ministry
#6

BRUCE G. EPPERLY

Energion Publications
Gonzalez, Florida
2020

Copyright © 2020, Bruce G. Epperly

Unless otherwise noted, all Scripture quotations are from the Revised Standard Version of the Bible, copyright © 1946, 1952, and 1971 National Council of the Churches of Christ in the United States of America. Used by permission. All rights reserved worldwide.

Scriptures marked "The Message" are taken from The Message. Copyright © 1993, 1994, 1995, 1996, 2000, 2001, 2002. Used by permission of NavPress Publishing Group.

Cover Image: Katherine Gould Epperly

ISBN: 978-1-63199-515-6
eISBN: 978-1-63199-517-0

Library of Congress Control Number: 2020939767

Energion Publications
PO Box 841
Gonzalez, FL 32560
http://www.energionpubs.com
pubs@energion.com

Table of Contents

	Series Preface	v
	First Glimpses	vii
1	Church Ahead	1
2	You Can't Go Back to Mayberry!	13
3	Making Peace with Pluralism	19
4	Choosing Life in a Death-Filled World	29
5	A Twenty-First Century Rummage Sale	37
6	Mystics in the Making!	45
7	A New Great Awakening	51
8	Theology Matters	55
9	Living Words: Finding Guidance in the Words of Scripture	63
10	Spirit Sightings	79
11	Worship Inspiring Wonder	91
12	Healing Hands of Jesus	99
13	Prophetic Healing	107
14	All Who Wander Are Not Lost	115

Series Preface

Clergy, having left Seminary, quickly discover that there is much about congregational ministry that they never learned in school. They may have touched upon the subject at hand in a practical ministry or preaching class, while an internship may have allowed a person to get their feet wet, but as important as this foundational education is, there is much that must be learned on the job. It is not until one spends actual time in congregational ministry that one's strengths and weaknesses are revealed. Continuing education is, therefore, a must. Having collegial relationships is also a must. Who else but other clergy truly understand the demands of this vocation? In addition to ongoing continuing education and collegial relationships, it is helpful to have access to books and articles authored by experienced clergy.

This series of books, the second to be sponsored by the Academy of Parish Clergy, is designed to provide clergy with resources written by practitioners—that is by people who have significant experience with ministry in local congregations. The authors of these books may have spent time teaching at seminaries or as denominational officials, but they also know what it means to serve congregations.

The Academy of Parish Clergy, the sponsor of this book series, was founded in the late 1960s. It emerged at a time when clergy began to see themselves as professionals—on par with physicians and attorneys. As such, they not only welcomed the status that comes with professional identity, but they also embraced the concept of professional standards and training. As they embraced professional status, it was understood that clergy would not only obtain graduate degrees (such as the Master of Divinity), but they were to engage in ongoing continuing education. Following the lead of other professions, the founders of the Academy of Parish Clergy saw this new organization as the equivalent to the American Medical Association or the American Bar Association. By becoming a member of this organization, one would have access to a set of standards, a means of accountability outside denominational auspices, and have access to continuing education opportunities. These ideals remain in place to this day. The Academy stands as a beacon to clergy looking for support and accountability in an age when even the religious vocation is no longer held in high esteem.

In 2012, the Academy launched its first book series in partnership with Energion Publications. This series was titled *Conversations in Ministry*, which fits closely with an important part of the mission of the Academy. That purpose involves encouraging clergy to gather in groups for mutual support and accountability in their local ministry settings. The books in this first series are brief (under 100 pages), making them useful for igniting conversation.

This second series, *Guides to Practical Ministry*, features longer books. Like the books in the first series, these books are primarily written by clergy for clergy. They can be used by groups in much the same way as the first series, but because they are lengthier in scope, they allow for greater depth. Books in this series will cover issues such as sermon preparation, interim ministry, self-care, clergy ethics, administrative tasks, the use of social media, worship leadership, and preaching on special issues.

On behalf of the Academy of Parish Clergy, the editorial team for the series, and the publisher, I pray that the books in this series will be a blessing to all who read them.

Robert D. Cornwall, FAPC
General Editor

FIRST GLIMPSES

One of the great joys of my life is being a pastor-theologian in just such a time as this. This is not an easy time for the pastors and their congregations, but it is exciting. The times call us to higher creativity and deeper spirituality. They call us, as God called Celtic pilgrims, to venture out on the high seas of faith, often without compass, map, or rudder. The waters of twenty-first century spirituality are uncharted and our maps are being revised daily. Still, God's mercies are new every morning, and for those who train their spiritual senses there are landmarks along the way.

I renewed my Christian faith as a college student during the Vietnam War. I felt the call to integrate academic and ordained ministry a few years later as a Ph.D. student at Claremont Graduate University. I wanted to give something back to the progressive church whose openness enabled me to claim the identity as "Christian" despite the theological deconstruction of my childhood faith.

My spiritual journey parallels that of many of today's baby boomers. For a generation, raised in the stability of the 1950s everything was up for grabs by the time we entered college in the 1960s and '70s. Mired in the war in Vietnam, we discovered that we Americans were the enemy, as the comic strip "Pogo" aptly noted. We also found out that the affirmation "liberty and justice for all" more often applied to white males than to women and persons of color. Shortly thereafter, we discovered what had been true, but hidden throughout American history, the reality that often our nation's leaders couldn't be trusted to have our best interests in mind or place national well-being over personal aggrandizement or ideology. Vietnam, Watergate, the Summer of Love, and the deaths of Robert Kennedy and Martin Luther King changed everything for millions in my generation. We forged our own paths, thinking we could change the world, only to discover on the verge of retirement forty years later what a mess we've made of things. We distrusted institutions and then led them, only to embrace the qualities we disparaged in our parents' generation. We "invented" the ecological movement and then destroyed the environment by our thoughtless consumption and materialism. We believed we could "have it all," not realizing the finitude of the planet that gave us life.

Now in our 60's and early 70's, we have much to repent. To our chagrin, we have discovered that we Americans are again the enemy as our leaders turn their backs on responding to global climate change, choosing profits over the words of the prophets. We lament that our nation still remains at the top in terms of consumption and pollution. To our surprise, we also find ourselves as leaders of the churches we abandoned as irrelevant forty years before. We realize that beyond repentance, there must be action to confront the interdependent realities of climate change, consumerism, the growing gap between the rich and poor, cultural polarization, racism, and misogyny.

Baby boomers have discovered mortality and as sunset is coming to our generation, we need to simultaneously guide and let go of institutional control while mentoring future generations of church leaders. We need to repent our loss of idealism and capitulation to the social mores we once challenged, while recognizing that we still have a vocation to become creators along with our successors of new paths of spiritual transformation. For those of us still involved in the church, and there are fewer of us every year, we need to look for signs of an imaginative and agile church on the horizon. Our boomer contemporaries write of "spiritual migration," "a new great awakening," "the great emergence," and "Christianity after religion," seeing these as signs of a hopeful future. But, we must live into these possibilities. We must put these insights into practice as we seek to join God in breathing new life into the dry bones of today's Christianity.

The meditations in this text are simply that — short meditations, grounded in my experience as a congregational and university pastor, seminary professor, and spiritual pilgrim - and not a systematic theology or a comprehensive "how-to" book on church vitality and mission (while these are on occasion valuable and many quite inspirational, they never fully respond to the needs and passions of particular pastors and congregations). Still, I believe that congregations can experience spiritual transformation. I believe that beyond the dead ends we imagine for the church lie new horizons and that, if we open to God's Spirit, God can still make a way where we previously believed there was no way. That is my hope as I write these words. That hope inspires me to share my thoughts as a pastor verging on my late 60's, not ready to retire, but inspired to share my hopes for new life and growth in an age of cultural and spiritual upheaval.

This text is political in the sense that theology and public policy are intimately connected to our vision of reality, values, and personal and institutional behaviors. Prophets and sages rooted their insights in their own time and place, whether that was the time of Uzziah, Jeroboam, Augustus, or Tiberius. Each of these national leaders as well as our current political leaders brought seismic shifts in culture and governance, and so does the leadership of our time. In the spirit of our prophetic predecessors, the meditations contained in this book emerge in the concrete realities of responding faithfully to the machinations of political leaders bound and determined to make America great at the cost of destroying the environment, favoring the rich over the poor, saber-rattling, turning their back on traditional alliances that have given stability to the world, and only further marginalizing women, the GLBTQ+ community, persons of color, and immigrants and their children. What is important to the church of the future is that much of these retrograde movements are being championed by persons who claim to be guardians of Christian orthodoxy! Persons under 55, variously described as Generation-X and Millennials, already absent from the church, are becoming even more alienated from the church as a result of the pronouncements of perorations of conservative Christian leaders, who have compromised the Jesus' message of radical inclusion and hospitality to achieve their political agenda.

I also write this text as a congregational pastor as well as theologian, who must as pastor of a diverse congregation look for common ground among persons with diverse theological and political viewpoints. Each Sunday, I "thread the needle" between the prophetic and pastoral as I preach to my politically diverse Cape Cod congregation, aiming at shared values of compassion, hospitality, care for the environment, and concern for the vulnerable.

The progressive and mainstream church seems an unlikely challenger to such political and cultural destruction, but currently marginalized progressive, emerging, and open-spirited churches must be champions of the values of earth-care, justice, and compassion. They must pray, but also picket and protest our nation's failure to live up to its ideals. Once at the center of American society, the progressive, mainstream, and liberal church has been pushed to the edges. Finding a vital mission won't be easy for our aging congregations and we will need flexible and constantly replenished spiritual toolkits to forge ahead. We will need lively visions and practices to embody them. We will need to remember that small actions can transform the world, when performed by groups of committed followers of Jesus.

In the chapters ahead, I share my own tentative vision, in process and incomplete, but with enough light, based on over forty years of teaching and ministry, to provide one path to the future. I share these meditations and spiritual practices for your congregation and your personal reflections as a pastor or congregational leader.

I dedicate this text to progressive and open-spirited congregations and pastors everywhere, and to the congregation I pastor, South Congregational Church, United Church of Christ, Centerville, Massachusetts, where we struggle to join tradition and novelty in faithfulness to God's ongoing call to faithful adventure. I am grateful for the commitment of my congregation to be faithful in its time and place and to the insights of colleagues and friends, Brian McLaren, Doug Pagitt, Diana Butler Bass, Carol Howard Merritt, Jay McDaniel, Monica Coleman, Patricia Adams Farmer, and Eric Elnes. I want to thank my Wesley Theological seminar, "Spiritual Practices for Ministerial and Congregations," and the committed pastors who made up this seminar, Kelly Grimes, Elena Melnikova, and Tim Tutt as well as Lew Parks and Sara Sheppard who invited me to teach the class and allowed such an intimate class to be held in May 2017. I am grateful to my own mentors in church and classroom, some of whom have joined the "cloud of witnesses" — Marie Fox, Richard Keady, John Akers, George "Shorty" Collins, Howard Thurman, Allan Armstrong Hunter, John Cobb, David Ray Griffin, Bernard Loomer, and my faithful pastor-father Everett Epperly, whose example still lives on in my quest, "first, to be a pastor." Of course, I am grateful to Henry and Jody Neufeld and Chris Eyre at Energion Publications and to my colleagues in the Academy of Parish Clergy for their faithfulness in providing recourses for congregational and ministerial transformation. I dedicate this book to my mentors, students, friends, and congregants along with my two grandchildren that they have a vital, world-affirming faith, and continue to live in a planet of wonder and beauty.

A Note on this Text: This book was completed several months before the emergence of the Coronavirus pandemic, which shuttered public worship in North America and the British Isles. The pandemic exacerbated the challenges congregations face and now calls us to novel responses to the significant changes in our spiritual, political, economic, and cultural environment. If we are to flourish as a church beyond pandemic, we must commit ourselves to constant reformation and openness to God's vision of Shalom. While I have added only a few allusions to the global COVID-19 pandemic, I believe that beyond the pandemic, it is imperative that congregations and their leaders claim our vocation as God's partners in healing the world.[1]

---

1 For more on the pandemic, see Bruce Epperly, *Faith in a Time of Pandemic* (Gonzales, FL: Energion Publications, 2020 and my upcoming Hope Beyond Pandemic (Gonzales, FL: Energion Publications, 2020).

CHAPTER ONE

CHURCH AHEAD

> *In the year that King Uzziah died, I saw the Lord sitting on a throne, high and lofty; and the hem of his robe filled the temple. Seraphs were in attendance above him; each had six wings: with two they covered their faces, and with two they covered their feet, and with two they flew. And one called to another and said: "Holy, holy, holy is the LORD OF HOSTS; the whole earth is full of his glory."*
>
> *The pivots on the thresholds shook at the voices of those who called, and the house filled with smoke. And I said: "Woe is me! I am lost, for I am a man of unclean lips, and I live among a people of unclean lips; yet my eyes have seen the King, the LORD OF HOSTS!"*
>
> *Then one of the seraphs flew to me, holding a live coal that had been taken from the altar with a pair of tongs. The seraph touched my mouth with it and said: "Now that this has touched your lips, your guilt has departed and your sin is blotted out." Then I heard the voice of the Lord saying, "Whom shall I send, and who will go for us?" And I said, "Here am I; send me!"* (Isaiah 6:1-8)

Historical events can be bellwethers for the movements of God's Spirit. God works in the moral arc of history and responds to our political decision-making with new and challenging possibilities. God doesn't choose our leaders, but God is always seeking the highest good whether our leader is Obama, Trudeau, May, or Trump. The political and, I contend, the spiritual landscapes changed with the election of Donald Trump and Great Britain's decision to leave the European Economic Union. The repercussions of these decisions will transform our understanding of national sovereignty, global loyalty, and the role of the church as cheerleader or prophet for decades to come. Our era is not unlike that of the prophet Isaiah.

"On the weekend Donald Trump was inaugurated as the forty-fifth President of the United States," many Christians came to worship, uncertain of our nation's future and anxious about the changes the new president would make. Some were elated at his promise to "make America great again" and restore the traditional values of white heterosexual America and American military power abroad. Others, including many pastors, missed Sunday services due to their participation in Women's Marches across the country. In most progressive and mainline churches there was a feeling that our nation had lost its moral compass and was moving backward as a result of the promises of the President and the majority party to turn back the clock on GLBT rights, equality for women, affirmation of ethnic diversity, health care for the vulnerable, immigration policies, and response to global climate change. America's new president saw his election as a mandate for nation-first regardless of global consequences. For many congregants and pastors, lamentation, not celebration, characterized their spiritual ruminations.

Not expecting anything special on Sunday morning as they entered the sanctuary, and simply looking for consolation and a moment's respite from the 24/7 cable news cycle as well as their own spiritual despair, some congregants and pastors heard voices, quietly whispering, others saw visions, illuminating their paths, still others felt the foundations of faith shaking and the church they loved under siege. Some felt nothing but shock and despair at what they believed would lie ahead for the United States and the planet. Still others sought to reach out across the aisle, without judgement, condescension or rancor, toward those whose viewpoints radically differed from their own. Beneath all these experiences was an invitation from the All-Loving One, whispering: "What is your calling as a spiritual leader in this time of national upheaval? In this time, when leaders have lost their moral compass and the nation's future is in doubt, what is your congregation's vocation? Where should the church stand in a time of national and planetary upheaval?"

In the darkest nights, our vision focuses and we discover a light gently shining and seeds of possibility slowly growing. We may hear voices we have long neglected, echoing deep within our spirits, calling us to account and presenting us with an unexpected vision and more surprising question: "Whom shall I send, and who will go for us?"

Like Isaiah, we may want to run for cover when we catch a glimpse of the Holy One. God is, as C.S. Lewis says of the Christ-figure Aslan, never safe, although God is always very good. The "most moved mover," whose providence is moving in all things, God may shake things up to make way for new visions and practices. Encountering the Holy One, we may be convicted of our own apathy and complacency and our nation's contentment with injustice and inequality. We may listen, for the first time, to the fears of our Muslim neighbors and the undocumented immigrants who mow our lawns, clean our hotel rooms, harvest our food, and build our homes. We may have been silent as glaciers collapsed, massive icebergs split into the Atlantic, seas rose, and species died. We may have thought that severe weather had nothing to do with human-influenced climate change. We may have changed the channel as we heard reports of First Americans protecting sacred land from the manifest destiny of American greed. We may have felt helpless as we read accounts of genocide in Africa, Iraq, and Syria. We may have been uncomfortable with what we perceive to be the radical messages of the "Occupy," "Me, too!" and "Black Lives Matter" movements despite the truths embedded in their protests. We may have felt disenfranchised as governmental policies and cabinet choices appeared hell-bent on turning back the ethical clock to the 1950s, normalizing racism and cyber-bullying, privileging fundamentalist Christian exceptionalism in science and the schools, and advocating short-term profit over long-term planetary well-being. We may also, for the first time, have heard the voices of those others who celebrated nation first on both sides of the Atlantic and saw Donald Trump as the last hope for the United States or recognized the fear, motivating white supremacy marchers in Charlottesville and realized that they too are God's beloved children. But, "in the year Donald Trump was inaugurated as President," — and, I suspect, in the years lying beyond Trump's administration - we were awakened from our malaise and despair by the divine questions, "Who will speak for the vulnerable, lost, and neglected? Who will speak for the Earth? Who will call for facts and not falsehoods?" As theologian and pastor Eric Elnes asserts, there are gifts hidden in the dark wood; there is wisdom in the chaos and guidance in the storm.

The Biblical witness is always historical. Christian faith is always contextual and personal, and never abstract or timeless. We are faithful — or unfaithful — in our time and place, and no other. God's Gentle Providence — and sometimes Challenging Demand — is always just for time like this, in our moment, our nation and our planet. To many of us, the old order is rapidly collapsing — spiritually, politically, economically, and ecologically, and the dream of a new and healthier world is far off on the horizon, luring us forward, but with no guarantee of achievement. We are both anxious and excited about the realities that will confront us and our planet in the years to come. We know the path ahead is uncertain, and even as we champion our causes, we want to reach out to those with profoundly different solutions to our national and planetary crises.

There's nothing new about national and international chaos, especially as we reflect on the biblical witness. The future is always undecided, even for God, and the future always calls us forward, despite the opaqueness of what lies ahead. Yet, for just such a time as this, we may like Queen Esther, discover our calling to be participants in saving our nation from its own foolishness and bringing beauty to a threatened planet.

GLIMPSES OF THE CHURCH AHEAD OF US

This book emerged from an unexpected vision. Driving around on a rural road in North Truro on the outer edge of Cape Cod, Massachusetts, I noticed a road sign for the first time. Although I had driven past it many times while traveling with my wife to

Christian Union Church in North Truro, where she served as pastor, I had never really seen it. I wonder how many other travelers had also been oblivious to the announcement "Church Ahead." I am sure that the sign was intended to be a wakeup call to drivers, reminding them to slow down to ensure the safety of congregants crossing the street. But, that day, it meant something more than protection for pedestrians. It was as if God whispered in my ear, "Church Ahead! Look deeper at your life and your vocation. What is the church that lies ahead for us? Will we miss it or will we be partners in creating Church Ahead, the church not yet born, but luring us toward new horizons of faithfulness and commitment? How will we respond to God's invitation to mission in the second and third decades of the twenty-first century? How will we keep the faith and join heart, head, and hands in the years ahead?"

Martin Luther King once challenged the church to be a headlight rather than a tail light in addressing the critical issues of our time. King realized that looking backward — and trying to turn back the clock can be comforting to those who are homesick for the good old days — for a less complicated time, for a world in which persons of color knew their place and GLBT persons hid in the closet, a world in which God, mom, gun ownership, the flag, and apple pie represented the best in America, and we could without any pang of conscience yell, "drill, baby, drill."

There is comfort in remembering the good old days and all of us need a Sabbath from life's complexities. Many of us long for an internet Sabbath, Sunday mornings where church and not youth sports are the primary focus of family life, and quiet days without the moment by moment crises of the twenty-four hour cable news cycle. We might even long for the good old days of President Barack and First Lady Michelle Obama, when we experienced dignity in the Oval Office, steady leadership, and the expansion of human rights. Some of us might even be nostalgic for the days of George and Laura Bush and George H.W. Bush and the decency they demonstrated in times of national crisis! As we hear cries of anger against our Muslim neighbors, we might recall George Bush's magnanimous words about Islam following the terrorist attack on 9/11. But, whether you are a progressive Christian like myself, member of the Sunday morning Starbucks and arugula crowd, agnostic seeker, open-spirited evangelical troubled by religious leaders whose politics betray the message of Jesus, or a conservative Christian, sporting an American flag and gun rack on the back of your pickup truck as a sign that you want to take back America from what you perceive to the growing power of gays, women, and minorities, you can't go back to yesterday.

All things flow. We can't step into the same stream twice, and perhaps not even once. Dreaming of an ideal past goes against the moral arc of history and God's own providential movements in our world. Though we can lean on God's faithfulness, we need to remember that God's mercies are new every morning and that God is always challenging those living in the past with the declaration, "Behold, I do a new thing!" As a theologian once noted, God's middle name is change!

A New Church and a New Faith

The meditations contained in this book are intended to provide inspiration for a particular audience: progressive and liberal Christians struggling to maintain a hopeful vision amid shrinking membership during a time of momentous change and disenfranchisement; moderate Christians who experience the same uncertain congregational, denominational, and national futures, but hope for the best with a change in leadership; evangelical Christians, who were unwilling to sell their souls in hopes of a return of Christian exceptionalism; and seekers and persons who describe themselves as spiritual but not religious and who are in search of communities where hospitality and healing abound and spiritual pilgrims can find a theological and philosophical framework within which to place their lives. While I have not given up on conservative evangelical Christians, and desire to find common cause with them, I realize that my theological, spiritual orientation, and values may represent what they perceive to be what's wrong with America and Christianity today.

We live in challenging, worrisome, and exciting times which call us to be faithful. As we ponder the church that lies ahead of us, we need to be willing to become God's new creation, to become new Christians for a new age or agnostics with a vision, and to recognize with Gandhi that we are the change we are looking for. Anxious over the possible dark time ahead, we would do well to remember the words from Harry Emerson Fosdick's hymn, "God of Grace and God of Glory." Fosdick's poetry can be a rallying call for peaceful warriors and imaginative artists arising to bring healing, share good news, and become companions in God's quest to heal the world:

> Lo! the hosts of evil 'round us,
> Scorn Thy Christ, assail His ways.
> From the fears that long have bound us,
> Free our hearts to faith and praise.
> Grant us wisdom, grant us courage,
> For the living of these days,
> For the living of these days.

> Set our feet on lofty places,
> Gird our lives that they may be,
> Armored with all Christ-like graces,
> In the fight to set[all] free.
> Grant us wisdom, grant us courage,
> That we fail not [all] nor Thee,
> That we fail not [all] nor Thee.

> Save us from weak resignation,
> To the evils we deplore.
> Let the search for Thy salvation,

Be our glory evermore.
Grant us wisdom, grant us courage,
Serving Thee Whom we adore,
Serving Thee Whom we adore.

"Church ahead" is a dream and a hope that will call us to our highest and best theologically, spiritually, relationally, and politically. We cannot resign ourselves "to the evils we deplore" as we witness what we perceive to be our leaders' abandonment of Earth care, preferring profits over prophets; exaltation of ideology over rationality; retreat from world-loyalty and global responsibility; worship of consumption and wealth; and promotion of polarization of race and religion. We must polish our moral compasses, and reclaim the ethical visions our leaders have abandoned, for God and this good Earth.

LAMENT AND AFFIRMATION FOR THE CHURCH AHEAD

A few months after I came upon the sign pointing "Church Ahead," I sat down with theologian-spiritual leader Brian McLaren. As I shared this project and the road sign that motivated it, he pulled out his cell phone and showed me an alternative sign, posted at a church parking lot:

Dead End.
No Church Parking.

We can move ahead or we can content ourselves with a self-interested, self-contained church, closed off to the world. In any case, the future awaits pointing to a dead end or a new horizon.

Singer-songwriter Bob Dylan once proclaimed that "The times they are a changin'." Surely this is true for mainstream and progressive Christianity. As we look at the demographics of our congregations, we recognize that our congregations are, for the most part, aging, shrinking, and troubled by reports of our denominational and congregational demise. Often, we feel hopeless as we look at the future of our congregations and the waning impact of progressive Christianity in contemporary America. As we look at statistics, we wonder, with the prophet Ezekiel, "Can these dry bones live?" But, as anxious as we are about the future, we may feel a breeze, a breath of fresh air, reviving and inspiring us to new adventures. In the dark soil, seeds germinate; small is beautiful; and from the smallest seeds great trees can grow. Perhaps, even in the "dark soul" - a typo in my first draft - seeds of hope will emerge from moist dark soil and from fragile and anxious beginnings realistic hope and compassionate challenge will emerge.

As we look at the current landscape of faith, we recognize that despite the death of Christendom, the whining of conservatives about the "war on Christmas" and the demise of Christian exceptionalism, God is making a way where there is no way, bringing new life out of what appears to be dying. We don't expect a dramatic Second Coming to relieve us of responsibility to care for the planet or shape our future. We have glimpsed the apocalypse and know that destruction and creation are in our hands, not the machinations of a distant, micromanaging, and vindictive God. What we look for is Christ coming to us as guide and companion as we daily navigate our pluralistic and polarized age.

We aren't alone in our quest for a life-affirming faith. God is with us. But, God needs us to be God's companions in bringing life from darkness, birth out of death, and abundance out of scarcity. Perhaps, in all our uncertainty and confusion, we are the Second Coming, the new creation, and the future church that we have been looking for as we discover that God and humankind need each other to be companions in healing the world. With poet June Jordon, we must claim, amid the multiple crises of our time, that we are the ones we have been waiting for; but more than that we are the ones that God has been waiting for to be companions in healing the planet and our communities.

There is much to lament. Yet, like the laments found in the book of Psalms, we intuit that within our lamentations is hidden a prayer for new possibilities and the energy to achieve them. In the wake of a forest fire, new seedlings burst forth, the hope of new growth. In a humble dwelling, the Christ-child is born. Out of death comes resurrection. With theologian, civil rights activist, and African American mystic Howard Thurman, we can prayerfully imagine a growing edge — "the birth of a child...the basis of hope in moments of despair," emerging when the world we once trusted is at risk.

All around us worlds are dying and new worlds are being born;
All around us life is dying and life is being born.
The fruit ripens on the tree;
the roots are silently at work in the darkness of the earth
against a time when there shall be new leaves, fresh blossoms, green fruit.
Such is the growing edge!
It is the extra breath from the exhausted lung,
the one more thing to try when all else has failed,
the upward reach of life when weariness closes in upon all endeavor.
This is the basis of hope in moments of despair,
 the incentive to carry on when times are out of joint
and men have lost their reason, the source of confidence
when worlds crash and dreams whiten into ash.
The birth of the child — life's most dramatic answer to death — this is the growing edge incarnate.
Look well to the growing edge!

Within our lamentations, we can experience the vision of new creation, and in all the turmoil of our lives, we can affirm with those who faced persecution for their faith, "how can we keep from singing?" Against the odds, and faith is always against the odds, we can experience God's graces and claim our role in healing the world.

In the chapters that follow, I will explore a lively, holistic faith for the future, that joins contemplation and action. I will reflect on the challenges of ministry, congregational life, social responsibility, and Earth care and present a humble, yet hopeful, vision of what our church ahead can be. God's future calls us. Look well to the growing edge!

Spirituality and Action for the Church Ahead

Each chapter concludes with practices joining contemplation and action, aimed at inspiring imaginative visions for the church that lies ahead. The path forward is paved with prayer. Congregations can actively move ahead toward new horizons, inspired by their commitments to personal and communal spiritual practices. These spiritual practices are aimed at moving your congregation forward toward integrating contemplation and action and theological reflection and concrete action. They also seek to inspire common spiritual commitments and experiences among persons with diverse political, social, and theological perspectives. Feel free to alter these practices of contemplative action to suit your personal or community's needs.

Spiritual Adventures. The first practice joins breathing, visualizing, and drawing. Breath is essential to life and growth. Breath expands while anxiety constricts. In this exercise, simply close your eyes and breathe slowly and deeply. Experience God's loving energy filling you with each breath. Experience the dry bones of fatigue and hopelessness springing back to life. Let each breath connect you with God's Spirit and the ambient universe. Experience yourself as part of one enlivening and inspiring breath moving through all creation. Experience your deep connection with loved ones and heroes of faith. Visualize them as God's beloved children.

At some point in the next few days, repeat this breath prayer. Once you feel centered and energized, allow your imagination to roam freely as you consider, without any restraint, your vision of the church that lies ahead. What would your congregation be like if God's Spirit enlivened it? What values, images, and mission would characterize your congregation if it broke through dead ends to embrace an open future? Experience God's loving light enveloping friend and foe alike.

Take a few minutes to draw or paint the church you have visualized, and ask God to give you wisdom in embodying the church of the future in some small way in the week ahead.

Contemplative Action. In this time of theological, political, and cultural polarization, we are called to be agents of healing and reconciliation. We are challenged to remember the words of peace activist A.J. Muste, "There is no way to peace. Peace is the way." We need to begin by spiritual reconciliation with those with whom we differ that will eventually lead commitments to specific common causes that cross our theological and political divisions. Return to the breathing practice, described above: breathe deeply your sense of connection with all creation, your family, and persons in your congregation. Now, breathe deeply your sense of connection with persons with whom you differ politically and theologically. Visualize them as God's children. Breathe deeply your sense of connection with political leaders here and abroad, perhaps the leaders of the United States, China, Russia, and North Korea, visualizing them as God's children. Pray that our leaders find guidance and wisdom in seeking the well-being of our planet and its peoples. Ask God to enable you to discern the wheat amid the chaff in the policies and practices of those with whom you disagree.

Within your congregation, consider ways to reconcile diverse viewpoints, theologically, culturally, and politically. How might this "holy encounters" begin? What one positive action can your congregation take to respond to our unique historical time?

CHAPTER TWO

You Can't Go Back to Mayberry!

> *The steadfast love of the LORD never ceases, God's mercies never come to an end; they are new every morning; great is your faithfulness.* (Lamentations 3:22-23)

Two of my many guilty pleasures in terms of television watching involve watching Hallmark Channel movies and reruns of the "Andy Griffith Show." In an increasingly complicated world, there are times in which I simply want comfort food for my soul. I want to retreat to bucolic images of homogenous small-town America and promises that after the first kiss, love conquers all. I know that these programs are pure escape. Beneath the façade of peaceful and all-white Mayberry was the North Carolina reality of Jim Crow segregation, separate but equal schools, voter suppression and poll taxes, and violence toward any person of color who stood up against the system. Moreover, after forty years of marriage, I realize that "it's complicated" is the best description of even the most creative and loving marriages, including those inspired by the formulaic Hallmark kiss. The same can be true of the healthiest congregations, where politics, perspectives on worship and decision-making, and personalities, make life "complicated." There are times when "love doesn't conquer all." If we take our marriage vows seriously, we know that eventually one of us will be on the receiving end in the relationship and that death and grief punctuate every healthy marriage. If we take our congregational well-being seriously, in light of our commitments to growth, creativity, and diversity, we will also have to commit ourselves to honoring the give-and-take of contrasting viewpoints.

Still, there is a part of us that would like to go back to Mayberry. Sometimes we need spiritual macaroni and cheese to give us respite from the more piquant flavors of contemporary life. My

Mayberry was King City, a small agricultural and cattle town in California's Salinas Valley. In many ways, small-town America in the 1950s was idyllic. Kids could wander the streets until dinner time without chaperones. Boy and Girl Scouts, Little League baseball, Friday night football, and church on Sunday morning were the warp and woof of life in our community. But, beneath the calm exterior were racist attitudes among certain townsfolk toward the "Mexicans" — and that was the polite description of the migrant and, likely, undocumented persons who worked the fields! The only black doctor left town because "he just didn't belong." One Jewish family lived in town, but they too left after only a few years. The wealthier citizens built fallout shelters, so that in the wake of a nuclear exchange, they would survive while their less fortunate neighbors would die of radiation poisoning. I am grateful for my small-town Baptist upbringing, but to be honest, I don't want to go back, nor can I ever go back, to that idyllic but ambiguous environment of my childhood. Today, conservative Christians who sing about the "Old Time Religion" splash lyrics on jumbotrons and play their favorite praise songs on computers and cell phones and livestream church services when they are on holiday. Despite the protests of those who claim unchanging orthodoxy, the medium, as Marshall McLuhan observed, has changed the message. Yes, there are times we need macaroni and cheese for the soul, but we also need Jambalaya, chili rellenos, and sushi. We need spices that bring tears to our eyes and antioxidants to strengthen our spirits!

Still, within our congregations and society at large, there is nostalgia for an idyllic Christian or American past. Some Americans believe we can go back to the Garden of Eden and Make America Great Again, if we wear a brightly colored hat, silence minority voices, send gays and lesbians back to the closets, check ID's at bathrooms, bring prayer back to school, and ban Muslim refugees. Such nostalgia is comforting at best and dangerous and malevolent at worst. It is ultimately destructive of the Christian witness, despite the bloviations of court preachers and political leaders. Feeling free to say "Merry Christmas," following the 2016 presidential election, won't advance the gospel message if Christians turn their back on legitimate science, data on climate change, human rights, refugees, and religious diversity.

As I write these words, the impact of the 2016 USA presidential election and the elections to come are seismic for church and state. On the Sunday after the 2016 election one of my congregants sidled up to me with a big smile on his face and exclaimed, "You know why I'm happy. Trump won the election." I shook his hand and said "I'm sure they'll be changes ahead for us," breathing deeply and recognizing that relationship often trumps politics in our pastoral relationships. Some religious leaders, like Franklin Graham, believe God was at work in the president's election, ensuring his victory. Others, like Pat Robertson, connect devastating storms with God's punishment of disrespecting the president, despite the documented connection between global climate change and extreme weather patterns. Yet, putting on the brakes in terms of change and diversity and gleefully saying "Merry Christmas" will not usher in God's kingdom, make the USA a Christian nation, or halt the breakneck pace of global interdependence. In fact, as philosopher Alfred North Whitehead asserts, the pure conservative goes against the grain of the universe. Life moves forward dynamically. You can't step in the same waters twice, and maybe not even once! Indeed, the dynamic movement of life — the ever-flowing stream of life some Christians seek to dam — may be God's saving presence in our world. In stopping the flow of life, we may be futilely and temporarily obstructing God's adventurous vision for our planet. As Theodore Parker, and later Martin Luther King and Barack Obama affirmed:

> Look at the facts of the world. You see a continual and progressive triumph of the right. I do not pretend to understand the moral universe, the arc is a long one, my eye reaches but little ways. I cannot calculate the curve and complete the figure by the experience of sight; I can divine it by conscience. But from what I see I am sure it bends towards justice.

God is the source of the moral arc and though the adventures of ideas may move slowly, as the philosopher Alfred North Whitehead observed, eventually God's vision will come to pass if humans listen and respond to the call. God is still speaking! God is still acting! Biblical spirituality affirms that God is moving through the historical process. God is the most moved mover, intimately related to each moment of experience as well as the broad contours of history. God's Gentle — and sometimes Challenging — Providence guided the Israelites to freedom, challenged unjust rulers in Jerusalem, presented an alternative vision of humankind in Galilee, and defeated the forces of evil on Easter morning. God's Gentle Providence, globally active, inspires healing and transformation in every faith and culture. While we may occasionally need to retreat to Mayberry or a monastery for moments of quiet contemplation, God's flowing streams of justice and healing propel us forward inviting us to embody God's dream "on earth as it is in heaven."

More challenging and important to us and to those who believe God rescues believers from the coming cataclysm is the reality that God needs us as partners in mending the world. God is at work in the world, but our prayers and acts can be the tipping in personal, national, and global health and illness, and life and death.

Today, we are all pluralists. We are all dancing with a dynamic God. Even those who champion Christian exceptionalism must share their message in a world of strangers in daily life, at the workplace, on cable television, and the internet, most of whom are quite content with their own faith traditions and see no reason to kneel at the altar of "orthodox" Christianity. Congregations and their spiritual leaders can take nothing for granted, including the faith of our children and grandchildren, many of whom have chosen to be spiritual but not religious or practice hybrid forms of spirituality, taking what they perceive to be best from a variety of faith traditions, rather than committing themselves to the religious tradition of their youth.

Now. nearly four years after the 2016 election and in the middle of a time of protest and pandemic, the challenges we face are spiritually, as well as politically, discombobulating, especially as we recognize that mainstream and progressive Christianity are now at the sidelines and not the center of today's religious movements. Yet, being on the sidelines — on the fringe — enables us to claim new spiritual frontiers without the institutional baggage of the past. While the way ahead may be uncertain, we can trust that God will make a way where there is no way. Out of the mustard seeds we plant in our time, a great movement, motivated by justice-seeking, hospitality, creativity, and adventure may emerge. We may discover that in doing everyday tasks with great love, we will become God's companions in healing the world. We may come to see the challenges of pluralism, postmodernism, and even fundamentalism as blessings inspiring us to articulate a lively, growing, evolving faith for just such as time as now.

The Church Ahead recognizes the insecurity and anxiety we feel at the rapidity of change but reminds us that God always makes a way where there is no way. The Israelites made their way through the wilderness. Distraught Mary Magdalene met the Savior in the Garden. Antagonistic Paul encountered Jesus on the way to Damascus. We may not know the landscape ahead, but we can trust that in the wilderness of our spiritual sojourns, we have a guide.

SPIRITUALITY AND ACTION FOR THE CHURCH AHEAD

Spiritual Adventures. The times call us to imagine "impossibilities." The energy of God flows through us. What was impossible in one era becomes normal in another. What was unimaginable when we were children, we grow into as adults. With death all around, and religious and political leaders reveling in enacting death-filled policies, we need to imagine alternative and life-giving visions.

In this individual or group spiritual practice, once again begin with breath prayer. After a few moments of centering, let your imagination roam free. Follow the pattern of your life as you consider: What unimaginable behaviors in childhood are normal now that you are adult? How did it feel to transition from one stage to another? What enabled you to make the transitions creatively?

Now, look at your congregation. Remembering that limitation or concreteness is the womb of possibility, what unnecessary limits has your congregation placed on itself? What dead ends can give way to creative possibilities? What impossibilities can your congregation live into as it awakens to its future? What "impossible" partnerships can we forge with persons of different faith traditions and theological and political viewpoints? What creative projects would emerge if you placed no limits on God or the gifts of your congregation?

Take time to bless the impossibilities that lie ahead for you and your congregation as you commit yourself to follow God's spiritual arc for your life and congregation.

Contemplative Action. Many congregations have almost entirely given up on responding to the current cultural context or the needs of their immediate neighborhoods. *Continuing the process of holy imagination, consider the spiritual, economic, and cultural environment within a five mile radius of your church.*

What do you perceive as the greatest challenges for congregational outreach? What do you perceive — and this may involve holy encounters with people in your community — the greatest needs in your neighborhood? What initial action might your congregation take in responding to a particular spiritual need and a particular economic need?

CHAPTER THREE

MAKING PEACE WITH PLURALISM

"Do not let your hearts be troubled. Believe in God, believe also in me. In my Father's house there are many dwelling places. If it were not so, would I have told you that I go to prepare a place for you?" (John 14:1-2)

When I was seven years old, the churches in my hometown, King City, California, canvassed the whole community to discover peoples' denominational identities. My father chaired the group and kept the 3 by 5 response cards in his home study. One afternoon, while my parents were away, I noticed the stack of cards, about a hundred in number, and overcome with curiosity I decided to read through them. The denominational names were all familiar to me — "Baptist," "Methodist," "Episcopal," "Presbyterian" — until I came upon a religious tradition I'd never heard of before, "Jewish." I still remember that one family, the Kaisers, that registered as "Jewish" on the town religious canvass. In small-town America, a white Protestant child could grow into an adult without having met a Jew or African American. In the fifties, Catholics were commanded not to enter Protestant church buildings and marriages between Protestants and Catholics raised eyebrows and broke up families. Will Herberg wrote of "Protestant, Catholic, Jew" as if they were the only options for Americans in the 1950s.

How the world has changed! Today, with a click of a mouse you can learn about thousands of non-Christian religious movements. The era of Christendom is over and we live in a pluralistic age. The whining about the "war against Christmas" is simply the dour acknowledgment among some Christians that the world has changed and they don't like it. Not even travel bans on Muslims, border walls, and the appointments of fundamentalist Christians to cabinet posts and the courts can close the floodgates of ethnic, cultural, and religious pluralism. The pure religious isolationist, and the America and Christianity-first proponent, is going against the tide of history, despite temporary success. He or she may possibly be going against the liberating movements of God. The stream of pluralism that emerged in the 1960s through immigration policies and interest in Asian religion has become a mighty river, shaping Christians as well as non-Christians alike. Many children of the church have discovered that they can choose their own religion and have aligned themselves with forms of Buddhism and Hinduism, or unintentionally become part of the fastest-growing sect, "none of the above." This can be a source of challenge and chaos, it can also be an invitation to growth and grace as well as new images of community and fidelity. Progressive Christians need not lament the emerging pluralistic culture. It may be an opportunity to foster spiritual practices in our congregations and a deeper ecumenism, which embraces the insights of our planet's lively spiritual diversity. Our commitment to spiritual and cultural pluralism may even challenge us to find common ground with Christians whose faith and politics differ from our own!

The Gifts of Global Spirituality

We are entering an age of inter-spirituality, or hybrid spirituality, in which people mix and match spiritual practices from a variety of faith traditions in to what Diana Butler Bass calls a "bricolage" to bring greater zest and beauty to their lives. Among Christians, the walls between faith traditions have come down as pastors cite Buddhist monk Thich Nhat Hanh on mindfulness meditation, churches welcome yoga classes, choir directors teach breath prayers from Hinduism and Buddhism to enhance choral performance, and everyday Christians feel little dissonance at joining their Bible studies with receiving reiki healing touch treatments, going to an acupuncturist, learning Zen meditation, or participating in a Sufi dance program. I regularly pepper my adult study groups and sermons with quotes from the Dalai Lama and Thich Nhat Hanh along with biblical passages.

I am a committed Christian, whose pluralism is grounded in my faith in Christ. My own daily spirituality includes centering prayer, Transcendental Meditation, walking prayer, and reiki healing touch. I am a better pastor and spiritual leader, not to mention more open to Jesus' path of wholeness and hospitality, as a result of encountering Hindu-influenced Transcendental Meditation in 1970 as a first year college student and Buddhist-influenced reiki healing touch in the 1980's.

Many of us believe that Christians are called to embrace a global spirituality, grounded in the wisdom of John's gospel, "the true light, which enlightens everyone, was coming into the world." (John 1:9) Christian fundamentalists beware: despite the darkness of the world, God enlightens everyone, without regard to religion or ethnicity. Wherever truth and healing are found, God is its source.

Adventures in Boomer Spirituality

My spiritual adventures aren't unusual among baby boomers. As a child, a pious Christian's negative response to my question about whether her dog would go to heaven led to the first cracks in the edifice of the conservative Christianity that had undergirded my childhood faith. The whole edifice completely collapsed in the late sixties. By then, as a teenager, I realized that the God of conservative Christianity was too small for my growing spiritual quest.

As a preteen, I experienced panic attacks whenever I entered the Bible-believing, devil-hating Green Valley Christian Church, an "independent" congregation where my parents chose to go after moving from King City to San Jose, California. I felt short of breath and suffocated by the narrowness of the place, physically and spiritually. Deep down, I knew something was wrong, and while I couldn't intellectually put my finger on it, I realized that I could no longer be part of the world of Christian exclusivism, fundamentalism, bible drills, and missions to godless heathens overseas. I now recognize that my experiences reflected my need to breathe deeply from God's unbridled spirit.

In high school, my spirit left Christianity even though my body was still compelled to attend church. I found spiritual freedom in reading Emerson and Thoreau, and the Bhagavad Gita and the Tao Te Ching. My spirit soared with the Beatles' "Sergeant Pepper's Lonely Hearts Club Band," the Beach Boys' "Good Vibrations," the Chambers' Brothers "The Time has Come Today," The Who's "Tommy" and "Baba O'Riley," and the mind-blowing sounds of Haight Asbury's Janis Joplin, Jefferson Airplane, and Grateful Dead. Mind expansion was the name of the game in the late 1960s whether through adventures hitchhiking along the Pacific Coast, cosmic conversations, Asian philosophy, or experiments with marijuana, hashish, or LSD. Yes, I inhaled and also "dropped," and I am spiritually better for it!

During my first year in college, I felt a yearning for something more than my own literary and psychedelic ventures could offer. My heart was restless for a spiritual practice that would bring greater peace to my life, refresh my spirit, and open the doors to the possibility of the enlightenment about which I had been reading. In search of a spiritual path, I showed up at the Transcendental Meditation Center in Berkeley, California, one Saturday morning in October 1970. In this former fraternity house turned ashram, I learned Transcendental Meditation and I was forever changed. I learned an Hindu-based spiritual practice that has inspired nearly fifty years of spiritual growth, including learning and practicing Christian centering prayer, Ignatian imaginative prayer, walking and breath prayers, reiki healing touch, and the sharing in the healing ministries of Jesus. My experience with Transcendental Meditation inspired me to quit using marijuana and LSD; it also inspired me to return to church — this time at an intellectually-questing, liberal, socially-active American Baptist church across the street from San Jose State University — and I've never looked back. At Grace Baptist Church, under the mentoring of pastors

John Akers and George "Shorty" Collins, I experienced the grace of spacious, socially-conscious theology and found my calling as a theologian and pastor. Now, almost five decades later, my faith is still growing and so is my appreciation for the wisdom of other faith traditions. I consider myself a "global Christian," animated by a close relationship with Jesus of Nazareth and the belief that wherever truth and healing are found, God is its source regardless of its religious origin.

My own spiritual adventures have informed my pastoral and academic leadership. Guided by the scripture and our calling to be "a house of prayer for all people." (Isaiah 56:7), our church on Cape Cod routinely has reiki healing circles, meditation classes, and welcomes visitors from all faith traditions. The wisdom of Hindus, Buddhists, First Americans, Taoists, and Muslims is invoked alongside affirmations of Jesus' centrality in our spiritual journeys. We can put Jesus first in our lives and then affirm that Christ is the way that excludes no authentic spiritual practice.

These days, one of my growing edges has been to see the light of God and fragments of truth in my Christian brothers and sisters, who dismiss my faith and politics as naïve, heretical, and dangerous to the future of Christianity. While their critiques have not changed my commitment to the truths of progressive and global forms of Christianity, they have inspired me to move forward in my acceptance of pluralism and diversity within the Christian family, including those who deny the truth of positions such as mine. Humorously speaking, a stopped clock is right twice a day! There is "truth" in my neighbor's "falsehood" and "falsehood" in my own "truth," as Reinhold Niebuhr averred. When I am prone to write off the "right wingnuts" of the world, I am reminded of a story told by one of my pastoral mentors, Gordon Forbes. A politically active pastor of a liberal church, he was taken aback when a woman asked him, "Do I have to be a Democrat to be a member of this church?" This query propelled Forbes to embark upon a spiritual journey: while he remains a political activist, progressive in politics and theology, he now recognizes the integrity of those who differ from him politically and religiously. His prayer life enabled him to gain a wider, more humble perspective on his faith and politics.

Beyond Doctrine to Experience

One of the characteristics of the post-modern world is its emphasis on experience. To many religious seekers, doctrine is dead and experience reigns supreme. People want to experience God, and not just hear words about God. The perorations of affluent televangelists and White House court preachers ring hollow to those who call themselves "spiritual but not religious" or the rapidly growing number of North Americans who describe themselves as "none of the above." Lectures about the evils of marriage equality, diatribes against transgendered persons, and laws about restrooms along with intellectually dishonest and ideologically-suspect denunciations of global climate change drive seekers of all ages, and most particularly millennials, away from doctrinal Christianity. They recognize that many of the leaders of "evangelical" and conservative Christianity have drunk the Kool-Aid, preferring power politics over the healing hospitality of Jesus.

Sadly, many of those who leave the church or find it irrelevant, if not immoral, lump all churches together as equally ideological and spiritually-vapid. This cultural reality is a challenge to progressive and mainstream Christians but it is also an invitation to creativity and hospitality. We need, as Marcus Borg counseled, to invite persons to see Jesus and our Christian communities with new eyes, as if for the first time!

Today, churches are challenged to become spiritual laboratories, places of spiritual experimentation in which seekers are invited to experience a Living God and a lively self. When the United Church of Christ states that "God is still speaking," its motto is an invitation to experience the holiness of everyday life and to see God's presence in movements toward inclusion and justice-seeking. When the United Methodist Church affirms "open hearts, open minds, open hearts," this assertion invites congregants and seekers alike to join in a never-ending journey to fathom the mysteries of God and the universe from which our lives emerge. When Unitarian Universalist churches proclaim "faith, freedom, reason" as central to their faith, this affirmation invites persons to see the quest for truth and wholeness as complementary, not antagonistic to the religious quest. When Disciples of Christ claim to be a "movement toward wholeness in a broken world," members proclaim a holistic faith the joins body, mind, and spirit, and prayer and politics to heal bring unity and well-being to all creation.

The promise of postmodernism is that we can experience God and so can our neighbor. A pluralism of experiences invites us to growth and not division. God is always larger than our images and we can never, as the Zen Buddhists assert, confuse the finger pointing to the moon — our concepts and doctrines — with the moon itself, the Ultimate Reality as it shapes our experiences.

Ironically, the emphasis on experiential faith challenges churches to explore life-changing and inspiring theological visions. Experience and theological reflection are the yin-yang of the spiritual adventure. The recognition that all theological visions are limited and incomplete does not require us to dispense with theology altogether. In a pluralistic, postmodern age, theology is more important than ever. From a negative perspective, humble theological visions challenge unhealthy theological perspectives. Healthy theology is like Lysol; it cleanses the mind from ideologies and falsehoods. While we may not fully know what is right, we can articulate what we believe to be wrong and unhealthy in terms of theological reflection. We can challenge doctrines, whether in our own or another wisdom tradition, that emphasize original sin rather than original wholeness, damnation rather than salvation, divine coercion and punishment rather than divine creativity and grace, and exclusion rather than inclusion. We can confront religious behaviors that marginalize LGBT persons, privilege the wealthy, destroy the planet, and join Christ and consumerism without succumbing to hatred or condescension toward those who hold these viewpoints.

Life-giving doctrines look toward an expanding and open future rather than backward to an idyllic and authoritative past. Life-giving doctrines also look toward God's ever-inviting horizon of grace and question images of a "one, true church," "final revelation," "apostolic succession," "infallible holy book," or "perfect human authority." Theologies of the future see God as a dynamic and interactive companion, whose goal is the achievement of beauty and healing through maximal human freedom and creativity. Many revelations are welcome and many experiences are affirmed in the context of an ever-evolving, constantly inspiring God. More important than splitting hairs over doctrine is the discovery of common theological and ethical values that bring healing and wholeness to ourselves, our communities, our nation, and the planet.

A Faith of Sufficient Stature

Theologian Bernard Loomer captured the soul-making possibilities of healthy religious experience with his image of S-I-Z-E or stature:

> By size I mean the stature of a person's soul, the range and depth of his love, his capacity for relationships. I mean the volume of life you can take into your being and still maintain your integrity and individuality, the intensity and variety of outlook you can entertain in the unity of your being without feeling defensive or insecure. I mean the strength of your spirit to encourage others to become freer in the development of their diversity and uniqueness.[2]

In the integration of spiritual experience and theological stature, life-giving theologies inspire both congregants and seekers to find God in all things and all things in God. Churches that are theologically and relationally open-spirited provide a welcome mat and friendly companionship to doubters, spiritual pilgrims, seekers, and persons who have been traumatized by their encounters with

---

[2] Harry James Cargas and Bernard Lee, *Religious Experience and Process Theology*, (Mahweh, NJ: Paulist Press. 1976), 70.

religious institutions. In so doing, we not only make peace with pluralism but see pluralism — even positions antithetical to our own - as an invitation to imagine larger, more dynamic visions of God that help us to create a house of prayer for all people in which, as a church marquee in Washington DC proclaims, "all are pilgrims and none are strangers."

SPIRITUALITY AND PRACTICE FOR THE CHURCH AHEAD

Spiritual Adventures. Let us begin this time, with a time of stillness, breathing in God's presence. Let God's energy enliven your cells and your soul. As you breathe in, begin to accept the healing energy of the universe, God's healing energy and the giftedness of our planet and its people. Experience your sense of connection with the immediate environment, the larger community, and the planet as a living organism. In the spirit of the hymn, "Breathe on Me, Breath of God," experience Life as one great breath, joining you with teachers such as Mohammed and Buddha, Taoist sages and First American spiritual guides, and our Healer and Savior Jesus. Give thanks for the breath of God in all creation.

As you exhale, with each breath, blow a blessing out into the world, bringing health and insight to everyone touched by you, regardless of faith tradition. As you bless other faith traditions, feel your unity with them.

Try moments of breath prayer in corporate worship and at congregational meetings. A few minutes of stillness can open us to new insights from scripture and invite us to go beyond our particular positions to seek the greater good in congregational decision-making.

While it may be difficult, we need to extend this same healing blessing to those with whom we differ theologically, politically, or in terms of viewpoints on congregational worship and decision-making. Gently inhale. After a few moments, begin to visualize persons whose positions often "press your buttons" behaviorally, politically, or theologically. Take time, in the spirit of Jesus' counsel to love our enemies and pray for those who persecute you, to bless these people. Over the past year, I have taken time to pray for political leaders with whom I disagree, that they will gain a heart of wisdom and find joy in his life. In my prayers, I do not ask for a specific manifestation of wisdom and compassion. While it is uncertain that this has changed the quality of their behaviors, it has changed my attitudes toward them despite my ongoing concerns regarding their public policy positions.

Contemplative Action. Once again, exploring the five-mile neighborhood radius of your congregation, consider the following questions: *What racial, ethnic, and religious diversity do you observe? Does this diversity have an impact on your community? What interactions do you have with people who differ from you, politically, ethnically and racially, or spiritually? What action might your congregation take to deepen positive relationships with people from different groups in your neighborhood?*

Chapter Four

Choosing Life in a Death-Filled World

"I have come that they might have life, and have it abundantly." (John 10:10)
"I came so they can have real and eternal life, more and better life than they ever dreamed of." (John 10:10, The Message)

Poet Mary Oliver asks "what you are planning to do with your one wild and precious life?" Leviticus asserts that the ways of life and death lie before us, and counsels us to choose life for ourselves and our descendants. Choosing life applies to individuals, institutions, and nations. What is it that your congregation plans to do with its one wild and precious life?

Death is always an option, spiritually and physically, for persons and institutions. The ways of death, grounded in unbridled consumption and economic growth, are the primary goals of many North Americans, despite their impact on the environment. Political leaders want to roll back regulations on coal mining despite the obvious contribution of fossil fuels to global climate change. The quick profit, the bottom line, is our current government's top priority, though over the long haul these profits typically only benefit the wealthiest Americans, and completely disregard our obligations to the welfare of future generations.

The prophet Ezekiel once asked the question, "Can these dry bones live?" and then saw the vision of a divine breath blowing through the valley, reviving and vivifying what previously appeared to be dead. We ask the same question in our congregations and in our nation. Signs of aging are clear in our congregations, demographically and spiritually. Many congregants look back to the glory days of Christianity, the post-war era, when church, like Mom, apple pie, Little League, scouting, and the flag, were at the heart of the American ethos. Many congregants also yearn for the post-war glory days of the United States, promising to "make America great again," but are oblivious, or want to return, to the realities of racism, homophobia, nuclear threat, and wifely subservience, that went along with this image of American "greatness." Even the most powerful nation in the world can be a place of death when our priorities and policies promote global chaos, ecological destruction, nuclear holocaust, and fear among minorities. The "exceptionalism" we tout for our nation no longer applies to our moral vision, but instead relates to our exceptional disregard for the well-being of the planet, our fixation on short term profit to the detriment of communities, and our imperiling of future generations through policies based on climate change denial. No amount of pomp and circumstance can disguise the hollow souls of leaders who leave death and destruction in their wake.

At just such a time as this, how do our congregations become places of life? How do we become life-givers in a fearful national setting? How do we provide countercultural blessings, charting a path toward new life, while honoring the traditions of the past and listening to those who feel disenfranchised, whether Muslim mothers, immigrants, out of work Central Pennsylvanians and West Virginians, or inner-city youth? How do we heal the wounds of polarization and find common cause despite political and theological differences?

Surely, many of our congregations and their pastors need Spiritual CPR. Indeed, as the United States and other Western nations move toward individualistic isolationism, and a "me first" mentality, we are challenged to turn from our foolish ways so we can breathe freely and lovingly again. The body politic needs the breath of life and a new heart that comes from a type of Spiritual CPR. We need "we first" that expands our interest from self and nation to the planet and its many diverse people and species. That unexpected, yet graceful and undeserved, spiritual resuscitation is described by the prophet Ezekiel 37:

> *The hand of the LORD was on me, and he brought me out by the Spirit of the LORD and set me in the middle of a valley; it was*

> full of bones. He led me back and forth among them, and I saw a great many bones on the floor of the valley, bones that were very dry. He asked me, "Son of man, can these bones live?"
>
> I said, "Sovereign LORD, you alone know."
>
> Then he said to me, "Prophesy to these bones and say to them, 'Dry bones, hear the word of the Lord! This is what the Sovereign LORD says to these bones: I will make breath enter you, and you will come to life. I will attach tendons to you and make flesh come upon you and cover you with skin; I will put breath in you, and you will come to life. Then you will know that I am the LORD.'"
>
> So I prophesied as I was commanded. And as I was prophesying, there was a noise, a rattling sound, and the bones came together, bone to bone. I looked, and tendons and flesh appeared on them and skin covered them, but there was no breath in them.
>
> Then he said to me, "Prophesy to the breath; prophesy, son of man, and say to it, 'This is what the Sovereign LORD says: Come, breath, from the four winds and breathe into these slain, that they may live.'" So I prophesied as he commanded me, and breath entered them; they came to life and stood up on their feet—a vast army.

Can these dry bones live? Can our personal and corporate spirits be revived? How do we breathe deeply when millions are simply waiting to exhale? How do we become life-givers as congregations, when many persons in our churches and in our nation are experiencing shortness of theological breath and spiritual panic attacks? There is no obvious answer that fits every situation, but we clearly need to receive the breath of God to think imaginatively and creatively, and have the energy to reach out in mission, sharing the air we breathe with those gasping for air around us.

BREATHING SPACE

Perhaps, we need to learn to breathe again. When I first came to South Congregational Church, United Church of Christ, in Centerville, Massachusetts, I led the congregation in an experience of breath prayer as part of the children's sermon. I asked everyone to be still, close their eyes, and breathe deeply and slowly for a few minutes, and then queried how they felt. Children and adults alike spoke of feeling greater peace and calm, a sense of centeredness and intimacy with God. Even our lively younger children sat still as they inhaled the breath of life.

I have come to believe, based on experiences like these, we need to recover the simple art of breathing. We need spiritual CPR. One of my spiritual guides, Allan Armstrong Hunter, taught a simple breath prayer exercise:

> I breathe the spirit deeply in
> And blow it gratefully out again.

Vietnamese Buddhist spiritual guide Thich Nhat Hanh teaches a gentle prayer to accompany walking prayer and virtually every activity:

> Breathing in
> I feel peace
> Breathing out
> I smile.

What form of spiritual CPR does your congregation need today? Is it a greater sense of spiritual vitality emerging from a commitment to prayer and meditation? Is it a sense of connection which comes from praying with your eyes open? Is it the energy which comes from rediscovering your neighborhood and finding healing ways to respond to issues surfacing down the street from our church building? Is it the sense of direction that emerges when your congregation takes a stand on a pressing issue of our time — economic injustice, opioid abuse, ecological destruction, homelessness, racism and heterosexism, or immigration?

Although I practice contemplative prayer by drawing away from the senses, I have found greater spiritual depth and connection by praying with my eyes open. Most mornings as I walk along Craigville Beach, on the Nantucket Sound, I open my eyes to take in the beauty of the seashore, breathe deeply, feel my connection with all creation, and pray:

> God's light shines
> In me.
> God's breath blows
> Through me.
> God's love
> Flows through me.

I have also made a commitment to take a moment to pray for wisdom as I read the morning paper, check my newsfeed online, or watch the news.

First, we breathe, as a spiritual practice that moves us forward from self to world, and from holy breathing everything else follows. Dry bones wake up and dance. Dying churches are revived. Ideologues, left and right, discover connection in an intricate fabric of relationships. Distracted by the chaos caused by the machinations of politicians, we find focus from which to resist with strength and love. The Spirit goes where it wills, giving life everywhere, and no one can fully know its path, Jesus says. Spirit falls on a motley community of disciples and the barriers of language, economics, faith, and gender fall away. Inspired, we enlighten the world. Unafraid, we can move forward, guided by intuition, inspiration, reason, and empathy. We can be "thinking hearts," as Etty Hillesum asserts, whose practical spirituality can change the world.

In breathing with the Spirit of Life, we embody an alternative to the court preachers and whitewashed tombs of Washington D.C. We present a vision of a Christianity that is fresh, alive, and open-spirited, that welcomes everyone in a spirit of hospitality. Disillusioned millennials discover places where tradition and novelty, and contemplation and action, complement one another and experience a faith that joins head, heart, and hands.

"Everyone" means everyone! Recently, in response to the growing fear experienced among USA immigrants, law-abiding Muslims, women, and members of the GLBT+ community, we posted "God's house is a place of prayer for all people" (Isaiah 56:7) on our congregation's marquee. When I posted a photo of our sign on Facebook, one of my contrarian friends, responded,

"Trump voters, too?" In the spirit of spiritual resuscitation, the only answer is "Yes, Trump voters, too." To truly affirm diversity, we must be hospitable even to those who, out of conscience and study, disagree with us.

Choosing life in deathful times means welcoming everyone, even those with whom you disagree. Diversity must include the panorama of cultures, ethnicities, and spiritual traditions, but also the diverse flora and fauna of political and lifestyle perspectives. All are welcome in the peaceful realm, the community of diversity, where we move from opposition to contrast, and see diversity as an opportunity for dialogue and not destruction.

Spirituality and Action for the Church Ahead

Spiritual Adventures. Praying with your eyes open can enable you to see the everyday world filled with "God's grandeur," as Gerard Manley Hopkins proclaims. In this simple practice, begin with the breath. Breathe deeply. As you inhale, experience your connection with your environment. You are not self-made, nor are you alone. This moment of experience emerges from the universe within you and beyond you. Rejoice in connection!

As you sit or walk, experience the wonder of your environment. Experience beauty and holiness within ordinary things.

Now as you exhale, let your breath bless everything around you. Bless the flora and fauna, the hidden sea life, houses and buildings, animals of all kinds, and humankind. Bless your congregation. This simple prayer can be practiced anywhere, whether at work and play or during your congregation's worship service or board meeting. In breathing God's spirit, we find our spirits rejuvenated and our lives connected with creation its manifold wonder.

You can pray with your eyes open while watching television news. When you see the images of leaders from whom you are alienated, a white nationalist, a grieving parent, the leader of an enemy nation, you can take time for prayer, asking for God's peace to descend on earth "as it is in heaven."

Contemplative Action. Following Isaiah's affirmation that God's house embraces all people, consider the current demographics of your congregation, reflecting on the following questions: *What is the racial, ethnic, economic, and age distribution in your church? Who is present on Sunday morning? Who is present in our building during the week?* Martin Luther King once stated that Sunday morning is the most segregated hour during the week. As you consider King's insight, *do you think your congregation wants to be more diverse? If so, what might be standing in the way? What might have to change to be welcoming to a more diverse community? What initial action might your congregation take to signal your welcoming of diversity, whether or not it adds to your worship attendance or membership?*

CHAPTER FIVE

A TWENTY-FIRST CENTURY RUMMAGE SALE

The Quakers use the word "cumber" to describe the excesses that characterize our lives and stand between us and God. As I look in my closets and around my house, it is obvious that our family has too many possessions. I have literally thousands of books, clothes in my closet and chest of drawers I haven't worn for years and am likely never to wear again, unless I lose thirty pounds and bell-bottoms come back into style. Electronic mail, ideally suited for minimizing the use of paper, has only led to more printing, and piles of papers and files clutter my lower level office. I have four e-mail accounts that I have to check regularly to keep up with my personal, institutional, and professional relationships. Woe to the person who goes on a two-week holiday and does not check their e-mail daily! The abundance of things has led to a new profession — decluttering. It is patently clear that we need to simplify our personal and professional lives. We need spiritual as well as domestic decluttering. We may even have to simplify our congregational and theological lives.

Noted commentator on contemporary religious movements Phyllis Tickle suggests that the Christian church should hold a giant doctrinal and ecclesiastical rummage sale every five hundred years to rid itself theological and organizational detritus that stands in the way of its current mission. Tickle's suggestion begs the questions: If you were to hold a rummage sale in your congregation, what would you consider essential and what would you dispense with? What would you discard as unnecessary clutter? Looking at your personal or denominational theological baggage, what might you need to jettison as a hindrance to the spread of the gospel in today's postmodern, pluralistic age? In the wake of the five hundredth anniversary of the Protestant Reformation, we may need to travel light and be theologically and congregationally agile to respond to the unique challenges of our time.

While the list may vary from person to person and congregation to congregation, the need for spiritual decluttering is essential if we are to be faithful to God in our time and place. We need to simplify our spiritual and theological lives to rediscover the meaning of Jesus' message in the twenty-first century. While simplicity does not require us to jettison history and tradition, it does challenge us to prune the branches that choke the life out of the church and hide its message from today's spiritual pilgrims.

Decluttering the Church

As I write these words in the first week of Epiphany, I am already thinking of Lent. Ash Wednesday is just around the corner as a yearly reminder of our mortality and temptation to subordinate our relationship with God to self-interest and personal aggrandizement. Lent is the season of simplicity and letting go. Inspired by his baptismal experience, Jesus travels light as he goes into the wilderness to discern his mission. In their forty-year journey from Egypt to Canaan, the Israelites learned to follow God and let go of any other divinities. In Lent, we, like Jesus and his Israelite predecessors, need to let go of anything — however precious it may be to us — that keeps us from experiencing God's abundant life.

In 2017, people across the globe celebrated the 500th anniversary of the Protestant Reformation. One of the great positive events in religious history, the Reformation has also cluttered the world with unnecessary religious movements, doctrines, requirements, and denominations. It has also contributed to anti-Judaism, biblical fundamentalism, suspicion of science and rational questioning, and theological polarization. The unbounded grace of God has been imprisoned by rules and regulations, absolutes to be followed or believed at the risk of eternal damnation, all of which stifle the free movements of God's Spirit in human life and the world.

Although we can learn from our theological and denominational parents, we can't go back to Luther, Calvin, and the Anabaptists to find complete guidance for our time. We must move forward by grace, claiming the gifts of the Reformers while trusting, as they did, God's Gentle Providence to show us the way. The Reformed church is always reforming!

Poet Mary Oliver asks us to consider what we intend to do with our "one wild and precious life" as she describes an afternoon spent in graceful meandering. This same question is asked of our congregations and the spiritual movements that shape our lives. While every encounter is an invitation to healing and wholeness, we need to focus on what is truly important. Too many people have been driven from the church by boredom and frustration as well as judgmental and traumatic experiences. Today, churches need to travel light. While a decision-making process requires honest sharing of ideas, there comes a time when we must let go of minutia and get on with the business of being church. Churches show their irrelevance to newcomers and seekers when they spend months debating about the color of the carpet in the church parlor or how coffee hour should be conducted.

The Psalmist reminds us that wisdom comes from "numbering our days" and recognizing the preciousness of every moment. Such numbering is essential for the church's future. The Gospel is precious, and our spirits are precious, and should not be deadened by institutional cumber, when God wants us to be companions in healing the world.

Many congregations are on life support and are in dire need for spiritual CPR. Like a person with a life-threatening illness, we must choose life one day at a time. We must focus on healing and transformation and not become mired in activities that siphon our energy or take us off course. We must also repent, that is, recognize where our doctrines and institutional structures have been sources of racism, sexism, trauma, heterosexism, ecological destruction, and exclusion. We must turn around, take new paths, that promote healing and creative transformation.

The salvation of persons and the survival of humankind and the non-human world is at stake. As political leaders, many of whom describe themselves as Christian, seem bound and determined by their policies to accelerate processes of environmental destruction, sexism, racism, and international chaos, a strong and motivated progressive movement is necessary for planetary survival and human well-being. Moreover, as many conservative Christians gleefully align themselves with anti-intellectualism, climate change denial, homophobia, xenophobia, and misogyny, it is essential that progressive Christians provide a robust and living vision for seekers as well as persons within our own congregations. If we fail to speak up and share our progressive vision with the larger community, seekers will assume that our version of Christianity has nothing spiritually, intellectually, or ethically to offer them.

A Transformational Vision

We must begin with an affirmative vision, for without a lively, creative, relevant, and open-ended vision, our congregations and the progressive movement will perish. We need to focus on life-affirming and planet-transforming values and not outworn and incomprehensible creedal statements. We have lived too long with vacuous and historically irrelevant theological nostrums. As progressives, we have, with the United Church of Christ, asserted that "God is still speaking," and then provided little guidance to the meaning of this affirmation apart from challenges to traditional ethical positions. The postmodern emphasis on pluralism and experience challenges us to take theological reflection and spiritual practices more seriously as we offer a robust theological alternative to vacuous relativism and rigid fundamentalism.

I believe that vital religious movements dynamically and flexibly integrate a substantial and open-spirited theological vision, a promise that we can experience our theological vision, and practices to enable us to experience our theological vision. We need lively theological reflection and spiritual practice" to help us move forward toward the horizons toward which God calls us.

The church of the future needs robust, lively, and open-spirited theological visions. While there are varieties of theological reflection, the theology of the future must envision a world in which:

- God is alive, relational, and dynamic.
- God is involved in historical processes.
- God has a bias toward justice.
- God truly loves the world, both human and non-human.
- God is constantly inspiring us.
- God is empathetic, and experiences our joy and pain.
- What we do makes a difference to God. What happens on earth matters to God.
- The world is a dynamic, interdependent process, in which everything is connected.
- Non-human life is intrinsically valuable, even apart from human interests.
- We are God's partners in healing the world.
- Our calling is to do something beautiful for God.

Inspiring Faith

Lively theological visions can be experienced in everyday life. The open-ended vision I proclaim is grounded in the affirmation that God is the reality in whom we live and move and have our being. God is near to all of us and is, in fact, gently moving in your life as you read this page. God is as near as your next heartbeat, breath, or thought, and you can experience God's presence and then respond by doing something beautiful for God and the world.

Life-giving visions inspire world-changing practices. Lively progressive theology joins action and contemplation. With a sign at the Kirkridge Retreat Center in Bangor, Pennsylvania, our vocation is to "picket and pray" or, as Rabbi Abraham Joshua affirmed, as he walked with Martin Luther King, "It felt like my legs were praying."

In these challenging days — in our nation and in the world — we need to be both heavenly minded and earthly good. We need to join our prayers with prophetic healing, inspired by Jesus' prayer that God's realm be embodied on earth as it is in heaven and that all his followers, despite their ethnic, cultural, and theological differences, be one in spirit.

At the heart of progressive theology is a commitment to dynamic world-oriented prayer. We can connect with God's vision in moments of silence. We can feel God's pulse as we protest injustice. We can pray with our hearts, minds, and hands, knowing that as we love the creatures around us, we are also loving our Creator. We can experience God as we dance to a hymn such as "We are Marching in the Light of God" or "Let Us Talents and Tongues Employ."

A decluttered theological and ecclesiastical vision, focusing on shared values instead of inflexible and divisive doctrinal statements can creatively inspire healthy congregational spirit practices necessary to tilt our future from death to life.

Spirituality and Action for the Church Ahead

Spiritual Adventures. As part of the five-hundred-year post-Reformation rummage sale, individual Christians and congregations need to practice a reformed version of the Ignatian "examen" or "examination of conscience" that can be done individually or in a small group. After a time of silent opening to divine wisdom, focus on the following:

- Gratitude for the gifts of your faith and congregation.
- Areas in which your congregation has been most faithful to God, and has experienced God's intimacy.
- Areas in which your congregation has strayed from God's vision and obstructions that your congregation has put between itself and God's vision.
- Commitment of your congregation to repent of deathful attitudes and behaviors.

- Placing prayerfully your congregation's future in God's care, opening to God's vision of the future.
- Praying for ways to find common cause with more conservative Christians and begin the process of cooperative projects. (For example, a Habitat for Humanity build, a soup kitchen breakfast program, backpack collection for students experiencing poverty at local schools, support of single parents, worship with persons experiencing homelessness.)
- Discerning one step forward the congregation can make to be sharing God's good news, and taking that first step.

Contemplative Action. The Examen involves discerning our current spiritual condition and aiming toward a faithful future. Reflecting on what you learned from the previous spiritual practice:

Where might your congregation join with other congregations, bridging differences in belief and worship, to address a problem in your community? How might you go about identifying a particular issue and then reaching out to potential partners?

CHAPTER SIX

MYSTICS IN THE MAKING!

For "In [God] we live and move and have our being"; as even some of your own poets have said, "For we too are [divine] offspring." (Acts 17:28)

I teach a monthly seminar at South Congregational Church, entitled "A Month with a Mystic." Over the past five years, we have studied mystics from virtually continent and century in the century in the Christian era. We have also explored the wisdom of Jews, Buddhists, and Muslims. We have discovered as a community that God's revelation is not restricted to one race, religion, or continent. We have come to recognize that God's Gentle Providence touches all of us, regardless of our piety, orthodoxy, race, ethnicity, gender, age, politics, or sexuality. Even agnostics and people outside of organized religious traditions can experience the Holy. Often members of the class look quizzically as if to ask: "Me, a mystic? How can that be — my mind races from one thing to another, my faith is often weak, and I don't seem to spend enough time in prayer." Yet, just as God appeared to Isaiah in the Temple, unannounced and unexpected, during a time of political turmoil, God may reveal Godself in new and creative ways in our time, giving us both a vision and a task. God comes to us in our attempts to balance lamentation and reconciliation.

There are no prerequisites for mysticism. Anyone who experiences the Holy is on the way to becoming a mystic. Nor are there any specific models for mysticism. Some mystics are activists, others are poets, still others are monastics, many are radicals and others orthodox in their theology, and many combine contemplation and action in ways that change the world while others seldom leave home. Ordinary people can become mystics, simply by attending to glimpses of the Holy One amid their daily lives.

The church is called to be a laboratory for mystics and a greenhouse for spiritual transformation. This mystical movement is essential to its mission and social activism. Sadly, the church is often the place seekers — and the self-described spiritual but religious persons — least expect to find an interest in spirituality. They don't expect to find a focus on spiritual formation and healing in the precincts of traditional New England churches, but that's what they'll find at South Congregational Church and many other congregations, seeking to claim Church Ahead. To the surprise and delight of the spiritual pilgrims who enter our building or look at our website, our congregation sponsors regular meditation and healing groups, classes on centering prayer and spiritual practices, and reiki healing touch treatment for congregants and the community. Our Sunday service has generous times for silence and meditation accompanied by music. Congregants note prayer concerns, expressing their gratitude for the goodness of life as well as concerns about issues of health, refugees, and addiction. We aspire to be a community that is both spiritual and religious — a "house of prayer for all people" (Isaiah 56:7) that provides spiritual nurture, mission to the community, and intellectual adventure along with a commitment to the highest values of tradition. We are truly moving forward with congregational spiritual practices!

At the heart of progressive theology and spirituality is the affirmation that God is present in everyone's life and that our vocation as pastors and congregations is to enable persons to experience God's Spirit in their daily lives. Divine omnipresence means God is present everywhere — and that means that God's light shines and we can experience the Holy in the ordinary activities of family life, earning a living, taking care of grandchildren or an aging spouse, or being involved in local or national politics.

Many people believe that one place God is absent is in their own lives. They suspect that past behaviors disqualify them from an intimate relationship with God or that or that they must reach a certain spiritual level for God to speak in and through their lives. If God is present in all things, then we can expect that every moment

— and every person - reveals divine wisdom. Each encounter can be an invitation to spiritual growth and the healing of the planet. Every person, from a young child to an aging seeker to experience God's guidance, and beyond that even our companion animals and the sporting dolphins can be instruments of divine inspiration.

The Celtic Christian tradition sees the ubiquity of God's presence in terms of "thin places" and "spiritual friendships." Certain groves of trees, rock formations, or solitary spots were considered transparent to divinity. The Celtic Christians, along with their pagan predecessors, believed that God's presence shined through such "thin places," piercing the veil of time and eternity and making these spots portals to divinity. For them, there was no Augustinian dualism of nature and grace or creation and redemption. Grace glowed and flowed through all things for those with eyes to see. Creation is holy and despite human sin reflects God's wisdom in every cell and soul. If divine radiance shines brightly and uniquely in certain places and persons, it can glow everywhere. Christ became human so that we could experience our own holiness and discover that we, too, are the light of the world.

The Celtic tradition also sees divine revelation occurring in certain holy relationships. Described by the term "anamcara," holy relationships or spiritual friendships are windows into divinity. The face of my spiritual friend becomes the mirror through which I experience my own divine nature. We are truly one in the Spirit as God's Spirit is mediated through our own unique personalities and perspectives. Difference inspires wonder and partnership rather than judgment and polarization. Within the body of Christ, there are many organs, cells, and limbs, each of which has its vocation in bringing health to the body as a totality. When one part is healthy, it contributes to the well-being of the totality; when one part suffers, the totality is at risk. Mysticism, accordingly, seeks to promote abundant life in body, mind, spirit, and relationships.

Mysticism is lively and fiery. This translucent mysticism is described in the encounter between two North African monastics, Abba Lot and Abba Joseph, that illuminates our current spiritual adventures. One day, Abba Lot went to see the venerable Abba Joseph to seek spiritual counsel. "Abba Joseph," he confessed, "as far as I can, I say my daily office, fast a little, pray and meditate, I live in peace, and as far as I can, I purify my thoughts. What else can I do?" In response, his elder companion stood and stretched his hands towards heaven. His fingers blazed like ten lamps of fire, and he responded, "Why not become fire?"

Isn't that what the world is waiting for and what seekers are waiting to see? Congregations and Christians on fire for spiritual and planetary transformation. Jesus affirmed that we are the "light of the world" and that our vocation is to let our light shine to give glory to God and light to the world. In his last speech, Gautama Buddha counseled his followers to be "lights unto themselves" and we discover that inner light through the regular practice of silence, centering prayer, spiritual examination, imaginative prayer, and intercession. Yet, that inner light is meant to shine out into the world. Stillness leads to social transformation. Contemplation leads to challenging the forces of evil. Prayer leads to protest and protection of the vulnerable.

As a laboratory of the spirit, the Church Ahead provides abundant opportunities for silence, centering prayer, intercessory and healing prayer circles, healing practices, and spiritual movement through Qigong, Tai Chi, yoga, spiritual dance, drumming, and walking prayer along with more traditional Western prayer and contemplative practices. Each church will have its unique emphasis and specialty, but any church that wants to respond to the needs of seekers in the pews and in the larger community must provide some of these options on a regular basis. Spiritual formation should be as natural as breathing, and that includes intergenerational, children's and youth spiritual practices, appropriate to each age group. From this deep core of Spirit, we can then meet the world in its brokenness as we pray with our legs while calling our elected officials, spiritually centering with our hammers as we build houses for Habitat for Humanity, growing as we welcome persons of different races, incomes, and mental health conditions, and chanting hymns of liberation as we serve at the soup kitchen. In such contexts, our prayers may cut across theological and ideological barriers as we discover common cause in healing our communities.

We are all mystics in the making and our emphasis on spirituality will not only shine a light of welcome to spiritual pilgrims but sustains us for the long haul as we share in the challenging work of congregational transformation and national and community healing.

Spirituality and Action for the Church Ahead

Spiritual Adventures. Today, we begin with another exercise in personal and group spiritual examination. After a time of stillness, breathing in the fresh air of the Holy Spirit, let your imagination roam to those moments of ecstasy and self-transcendence, those moments in which we like the singer-songwriter Van Morrison journey "into the mystic."

Reflecting on your life experiences: Have you ever had — broadly speaking — an experience of transcendence or ecstasy? Have you ever felt that God was with you? What was it like to encounter the divine, even if God did not announce her or himself? What was it like to experience the "doors of perception" cleansed and then experience the infinite aspect of things, even if only for a moment? What did you discover in that moment of transparency to the divine?

As a community exercise gather in a small group for prayer and meditation, perhaps beginning with a reflection on Paul's affirmation, "In God we live and move and have our being." Take time to share times when you felt touched by God. Consider prayerfully the seekers within your congregation. What deep needs and passions are present among your fellow congregants? How might your congregation prayerfully respond to these? Looking beyond your congregation, take time to consider: What deep needs and passions are present in seekers in the larger community, including unlikely seekers such as single parents living paycheck to paycheck or homeless persons you encounter while serving meals at the soup kitchen or persons of different ethnic, cultural, and religious identities? Where is God directing you to respond to these spiritual needs? How might their spiritual needs relate to basic survival needs?

Visualize the personal and community needs you have identified, seeing Christ in the face of each person or group.

Contemplative Action. When we discover our identity as mystics in the making, each day we can open to the holiness of life by pausing to look deeper into the face of a spouse, child, or companion animal; arising a few hours early and gaze at a myriad of stars; pondering the face of a refugee child. Behold, God is here. A ladder of angels, ascending and descending, resides right where you are. You are at Beth-El, the gateway to God, as you march for immigrant's rights, stand beside a Muslim woman being harassed at the filling station, pick up a child at school, serve a meal at the soup kitchen, or walk on a familiar thoroughfare. Behold, God has a message for you: This world, the world in which you live, is holy and beautiful, and this world is your vocation — to love, to heal, to inspire. Mysticism leads to mission!

Recognizing God's presence in everyone, consider the following: *What groups do you find most challenging in your quest to see God in all people? In what ways can you deepen your experience of the Holy in these "others?" What one activity can your congregation undertake to be more pervasively aware of the "holy others" in your community?*

Chapter Seven

A New Great Awakening

*Arise, shine; for your light has come,
and the glory of the Lord has risen upon you.* (Isaiah 60:1)

The spiritual practices and mystical orientation we considered in the previous chapter are at the heart of congregational and personal transformation. Spiritually grounded congregations can transform their foci from individualistic survival to interdependent healing and hopeless reminiscing to transformational imagination. They can become fire and give light and warmth to the world. It's all about waking up to wonder and to the inherent power of small groups of people committed to great visions.

Hopeful commentators on the future of Christianity such as Phyllis Tickle and Diana Butler Bass assert that we are on the edge of a "great awakening." Others such as Brian McLaren speak of a "spiritual migration" focusing on values of earth care and incarnational living rather than inflexible doctrine or ecclesiology. Within the matrix of rapid cultural change and the collapse of Christendom, the political, social, and religious dominance of Christianity, in the Northern hemisphere, they see new horizons of spirituality emerging. Pushed to the sidelines by pluralism, postmodernism, globalism, and secularism, the church of the future can claim the margins as frontiers. No longer tied to traditionalism, "the dead thoughts of living people," the church can reclaim healthy and expansive traditions, "the living thoughts of the dead" and the aspirations of the "unborn" in light new images of God, spiritual formation, and congregational life. The church that lies ahead must travel light, opening to divine wisdom in unexpected places. While honoring the sacred places where we worship, our calling is to experience holiness everywhere. Affirming God's presence in all things, we can have an expansive vision, look for truth and healing wherever it is found, and share good news in ways that speak to the deepest concerns of seekers, pilgrims, and the "nones", and "dones."

No longer seduced by earth-destroying Second Coming prophesies, the church ahead looks for God's coming everywhere and in all things. While we trust God's Gentle Providence, we do not wait passively for a divine rescue operation or for God to defeat all our opponents. The many comings of God — and the so-called 'second coming," championed by televangelists and radio preachers - occurs each moment and inspire us to move from passivity to responsibility in shaping history. God calls us to be the change we are looking for in the world and to become God's companions in healing the world. God cannot — or will not — save our world apart from our efforts. In fact, our commitments enable God be more active in the world. We are God's hands and hearts and in our fidelity we open new ways for God to heal the world. In God's coming to the world — in contrast to the spirit deadening and earth-abandoning "left behind" images of popular Christianity — no one is left behind; healing is offered to all, not just once, but every moment of the day.

The new great awakening will be incarnational in spirit. The walls of dualism, polarization, and fundamentalism have come down, and the horizons of companionship with God lie head. "Cleave the wood and I am there, "proclaims the Gospel of Thomas. "The realm of God is among you," Jesus proclaims. The One who asserted "I am the light of the world" equally affirmed "you are the light of the world." The next great awakening is about enlightenment of the world, not just individuals. It is about finding revelation everywhere — in our cells as well as our souls, in the face of a Yemenese refugee or an undocumented worker, and in the wisdom of persons of other faith traditions. It is about hearing God's voice in atheists as well as believers, in poets and mathematicians, in conservatives as well as progressives, in Buddhist monks as well as Christian theologians. In opening to God's presence in all things, we will be awakened to earth as the most expansive revelation of divine wisdom. God is generous in God's revelations. It is we who have sought to build walls to separate the many avenues of truth. We need to wake up to God in all of God's glorious and distressing disguises.

Yes, wake up. Wake up to God's grandeur. Wake up to a new day, rejoicing. Wake up and with Maya Angelou "on the pulse of morning" and say with simplicity and hope, "good morning" to this wonderful world. We need awakened theology, spirituality, social concern, and worship. We need to say, "this is the day that God has made" and then "rejoice" in its unrepeatable, wondrous, amazing beauty. With ecstatic exuberance, we will rise and take our role as healers of God's world, speaking on behalf of the voiceless — the marginalized and the non-human world — and joining praise with protest to awaken the world to God's True Coming in this holy here and now.

SPIRITUALITY AND ACTION FOR THE CHURCH AHEAD

Spiritual Adventures. Rise up in body and spirit, and walk. Take up your life, as well as your bed, and walk. Let your senses roam with no particular focus. Simply be all eye, as a North African Desert Father describes the monk's vocation. Be all sense, tasting, touching, hearing, feeling, hearing, seeing, the infinite wonder of this moment.

For a moment, "consider the lilies" and liberate yourself from the apathy of consumerism to discover the ecstasy of sheer living.

As all eye, we see God in the lost, lonely, and forgotten. In seeing God in a variety of places, we move from wonder to transformation and mysticism to mission.

Throughout the day, give thanks for the wonder of all being and the wonder of your being. Let your attention move to certain spots, unbidden and yet inspirational, that lure you to one act of beauty and love one moment at a time. If our calling is to be God's companion in healing the world, what one simple act calls you forward now ... and later?

Look deeply at the persons you meet, opening to the inner light of God within them. Especially look at those whose "distressing disguises," according to Mother Teresa, reveal God's presence for those who look deeply into the faces of immigrants, undocumented workers and their "dreamer children," persons experiencing homelessness and addiction, white nationalists and abortion clinic protestors, traditional Catholics touting their one, true church and fundamentalist Protestants claiming they alone understand the bible. Somewhere in the darkness, God's light shines on all of us, yearning to come forth from captivity and ignorance and bless the world.

Contemplative Action. Building on the experience of "holy otherness," continue to reflect on ways your congregation can identify its "others," ethnically, economically, and theologically. *How might your congregation initiate sacred spaces within the congregation that address its own, often hidden diversity, and the more obvious diversity of the community? What one event might your congregation sponsor to demonstrate its commitment to addressing people outside the doors?*

CHAPTER EIGHT

THEOLOGY MATTERS

*Jesus answered: "You shall love the
Lord your God with all your heart, and
with all your soul, and with all your
strength, and with all your mind; and your neighbor as yourself."*
(Luke 10:27)

Today's church is called to think big. We are challenged, as the philosopher Whitehead asserts, to initiate novelty to match the novelty of our cultural, spirituality, and planetary environment. Currently, we live with the tension of the global and the local in government and ethics, not to mention the fact that our churches are being ripped apart by contentious perspectives about whether we should focus on immediate local concerns or emphasize the broader horizon of planetary and long-term issues. In truth, we must do both simultaneously. We must think globally, looking at the big picture and considering generations yet to be born, and act locally, doing ordinary things and responding to local challenges with great love. Healthy theology holds both the micro and macro and immediate and long term in balance. It invites us to see with a "god's eye" view that is incarnate practices that transform day to day life. We need to choose life for ourselves moment by moment and we need to see our choices as part of a larger story, God's vision of "on earth as it is in heaven," embodied in the slowly evolving moral arc of history.

Theology has a bad name among many Christians and seekers. Postmodern critics rightly challenge "large stories" because they often privilege the perspectives of the dominant and powerful — the status quo, the wealthy, the male — over those whose voices have been historically and are currently marginalized and silenced. Postmodern thought is also suspicious of any system that claims to have all the answers and reflect the experiences of all people.

Reality is far too diverse and mysterious for us to fabricate systems that fit all sizes, shapes, and cultures. Moreover, critics have rightly noted that our attempts to be objective and describe the totality of experience are often themselves limited and perspectival. Lay people have turned away from theological reflection in dismay, feeling inadequate as they attempt to read incomprehensible theological treatises or listen to theologians more interested in being erudite than communicating good news to spiritually and intellectually hungry people.

Healthy theological reflection must take into consideration both the *apopathic* and *kataphatic* streams of theological reflection. In the spirit of apophatic theology, we must confess that God is always more than we can imagine. God is a dazzling darkness that requires us to say, with the Hindu sages, *neti, neti*. "not this, not that," when speaking of the ultimate realities within whom we live and move and have our being. Humility is at the heart of healthy theology. Sin, self-interest, and finitude touches our doctrines as well as our actions. Still, we must embrace the *kataphatic*. The finger that points to the moon is aiming at something alive and real. With all our finitude and doubt, we must still seek to describe the Holy as completely, honestly, and faithfully as possible, employing the most spiritually evolved understandings of scripture, experience, tradition, reason, culture, and science. God leaves traces of divinity in us and all things and these inspire us on the quest for truth and healing.

Today, we need, with all humility, to frame big theologies and big ideas that are understandable to both Ph.D.'s and GED's. We need theologies of great size and stature. To repeat the words of one of my professors Bernard Loomer:

> By size I mean the stature of a person's soul, the range and depth of his love, his capacity for relationships. I mean the volume of life you can take into your being and still maintain your integrity and individuality, the intensity and variety of outlook you can entertain in the unity of your being without feeling defensive or insecure. I mean the strength of your spirit

to encourage others to become freer in the development of their diversity and uniqueness.[3]

We need theologies of stature that can embrace the wholeness and variety of human experience, holding in contrast the diversity of human experience while maintaining a strong spiritual center. In a time in which politicians seldom present us with big visions or call us to become better persons, we need theologies that challenge, inspire, agitate, comfort, and mobilize us for facing the willful destructiveness of the powers and principalities. We need theologies big enough to address our 13.7 billion year cosmic journey and intimate enough to respond to our personal experiences of despair and celebration. We need to be bold and yet humble in our theological reflection.

I believe that an open-spirited version of process theology is the best candidate to shape the future of progressive, emerging, missional, and global Christian visions. Process theology presents a constructive and creative post-modern vision, open to diverse cultures and experiences, as it presents a "big enough" story to help us understand our relationship with God and our fellow creatures. Process theology recognizes the relativity and finitude of every theological world view. Theology is always in process, always incomplete and subject to change and growth. Still, process theology boldly asserts that any open-spirited vision of reality can give us enough light for our spiritual, ethical, and institutional journeys. Moreover, theology, like spirituality, is constantly growing in stature, embrace, and insight.

At the heart of the process theological vision is the integration of theology, spirituality, ethics, and mission. Grounded in the earth and its rhythms and the currents of human experience, process theology challenges us to empathy and justice-seeking and calls us from the armchair and pulpit to be God's companions in healing the earth. Process theology is profoundly practical and salvific in nature. As one of my mentors, John Cobb, asserts, the job of the-

---

3   See page 26.

ology today is to save the planet and for that we need a planetary theology.

Theology is a series of inspirational and insightful affirmations reflecting our experiences of God and the world. Expanding on my earlier affirmations, I believe that progressive, processive, and emerging theology, makes the following affirmations, reflective of inclusive life-supporting, earth-affirming, and justice-seeking values:

- God and the world are profoundly interdependent: God shapes the world and the world influences God.
- God is present as a guiding and energetic presence in all things.
- God's presence in human life and the world is best understood in terms of possibilities that lead to abundant life, fulfillment, and beauty of experience for ourselves and others.
- God is constantly moving in and through our world — in the grand scope of history and in every moment of experience.
- God's presence in our lives is concrete and shaped by our decisions and actions. In the call and response of God and the world, our actions and beliefs either expand or limit the scope of divine possibility for us and the world.
- God's presence in the world is best known in terms of love rather than power. God's power is loving and relational, not unilateral, and dominating power.
- God aims at beauty of experience and the maximum amount of freedom and creativity, congruent with the well-being of the planet and the communities of which we are a part.
- God loves the whole world, with no exceptions, and that includes non-human as well as human lives. God loves endangered species, polar ice caps, and hammerhead sharks as well as Central American refugees, Appalachian coal miners, homeless children, persons with substance abuse disorder, and inner-city youth.
- Creation reflects God's glory and wisdom. Value and experience, and the ability to relate to God, occurs at every level of life.

As Psalm 148 and 150 proclaim, all creation praises God and everything that breathes can praise God. Accordingly, ethics pertains to non-humans as well as humans. Saving the baby whales and saving the baby humans are both legitimate ethical positions, and the value of creatures is not related to their specific species or valuation or benefit to humankind.

- All life is interdependent. All things are connected, from the divine and the angelic to humans and plankton. God is in all things, and all things are in God.
- Given the interdependence of life, what happens on earth truly matters to God. God feels the pain and joy of the world. Ethically speaking, this means that we are always faced with the question: Do we give God a more beautiful or uglier world, a world with greater love or joy or greater alienation?
- Our ultimate vocation as humans — and perhaps other complex species — is to be God's companions in healing or mending the world, whether in moment by moment acts of kindness, care for the vulnerable, or social and political involvement.

Although global in nature, these affirmations are intended to be poetic and partial, rather than literal and complete. We must always speak of God with humility. We must recognize the wonder and mystery of all being from the simple grasshopper chewing on a blade of grass, contemplated by Mary Oliver in her poem "The Summer Day," to the intellectual complexity of Stephen Hawking and the compassionate holiness of a Mother Teresa or Howard Thurman.

We cannot save the world on our own. Nor will theology alone save the world. We need hands and hearts as well as minds to bring light and life to the world. Often, however, we must challenge dysfunctional and false theologies that: focus on Jesus' Second Coming to the detriment of caring for the earth; promote disengagement from the rough and tumble world of politics and culture; encourage separation of mind, body, and spirit, and humanity from creation; claim to have all the answers and disparage alternative visions; privilege men over women, heterosexuals over the LGBTQ+ community, the survival of the human species over non-human species; support white privilege rather than the holiness of all races; prefer profits over profits and sacrifice the earth for short term economic gain. All these dysfunctional theological positions need to be challenged in light of the gospel vision of the peaceable realm, welcoming the vulnerable and caring for the earth.

Theology matters! Theology can change minds and change the world. Theology for the church ahead aims at healing, not destroying; welcoming not excluding; and loving not hating.

Spirituality and Action for the Church Ahead

Spiritual Adventures. We are called to love God with our minds as well as our hearts and hands. Over the centuries, the most inspirational spiritual leaders have also been theologians. Just think of spiritual and social theologians such as Isaiah, Amos, Paul, Pelagius, John Wesley, George Fox, Friedrich Schleiermacher, Karl Barth, and Reinhold Niebuhr as well as today's liberation and feminist/womanist theologians and spiritual leaders. Now, look at your own theological values in the spirit of a theological Examen.

Take a few moments for stillness, asking for divine wisdom. Then, in the stillness, reflect on the question, "What theological values shape my life? Are they healthy? What might I do to embody healthy, life-supporting, and spiritually-sound theological values?"

Then ask similar questions of your community of faith: Where do you observe theological reflection in your church? How would you describe it? Is it healthy or harmful, thoughtful or superficial? How does it inform your congregation's program and decision-making?

Close with a prayer for continuing divine guidance in your intellectual, relational, and ethical life and the life of your congregation.

Contemplative Action. Theology provides a frame of reference and inspiration for mission and social involvement. *Consider offering intellectually-accessible courses on how to think theologically or the theological movements in Christianity. Join these intellectual exercises with times of prayer and meditation. Invite members of the broader community to share in theological reflection with you.*

CHAPTER NINE

LIVING WORDS: FINDING GUIDANCE IN THE WORDS OF SCRIPTURE

Your word is a lamp to my feet and a light to my path.
(Psalm 119:105)

When someone declares that they are representing the "orthodox" Christian position on a controversial issue, I often reply, "which orthodoxy are you speaking about?" After all, virtually everyone's ancestors have been declared a heretic by someone claiming to hold orthodox views about scripture, doctrine, or sacrament. In the history of Christianity, battles were fought — some leading to death sentences, banishment, and excommunication — on issues such as the inspiration of the Holy Spirit, the scope of authorized texts, the power of God and the nature of human freedom, the deity of Christ, the nature of grace, and ecclesiastical authority. In some circles, the worst thing you can call a relative is to refer to them as a "Pelagian," even though Pelagius' vision of the goodness of humankind, the ability of humans to respond creatively to God, and the value of creation has inspired the revival of Celtic Christianity. Methodists and Presbyterians now get along and share in ecumenical mission projects despite the fact that the Calvinists, the predecessors to today's Presbyterians, deemed Wesleyan/Arminian theology's focus on our ability to freely respond to God's call a heretical position.

Today, many of us have eliminated the word "heresy" altogether from our religious vocabulary, preferring the word "heterodoxy" to describe the wide variety and often conflicting visions of faith held by Jesus' first followers as well as contemporary Christians. Those of us who assume the contextual nature of theology and practice recognize that every spiritual perspective is finite, relative, and to some degree imperfect in its description of God, freedom, nature, and human destiny.

This same dynamic is at work in our contemporary battles for the Bible, which have moved from the sanctuary to the courthouse, as Christians and jurists debate issues such as marriage equality, transgender bathrooms, abortion and birth control, health care mandates, teaching Genesis as science, and global climate change. While progressive Christians tend to recognize a variety of theological and scriptural positions, and opt for a separation of church of state despite their affirmation that our faith shapes our politics, conservative Christians implicitly minimize the separation of church and state, privileging particular Christian viewpoints in the formation of legal statutes. Some assume that the "war" on Christianity is the result of legal and cultural recognitions of science, homosexuality, and pluralism, although none of these directly influences congregational practices or the success of Christian marriage. Implied in this view of biblical truth is that certain Christians know best how to run our country, that deviancy from traditional norms should be ostracized, and the returning to traditional values and a traditional social order will make nation great again.

The role of scripture in evaluating science is potentially more catastrophic. As a progressive Christian, I am happy for the creation stories to be taught in a comparative religion course, but not in a science classroom. They not only are bad science, if taken as a literal description of how the world was created, but they suggest visions of creation that are at cross purposes with progressive and mainstream Christian's understanding of divine wisdom's presence in the evolution of the universe, our planet, and humankind. Beyond that, literal accounts of the Genesis creation stories limit divine creativity to a bygone era rather than seeing God as constantly creating in humankind and the non-human world. Moreover, the war on science, grounded in ambiguous scriptural passages related to the Second Coming, has been used to challenge scientific evidence of global climate change and weaken regulations on carbon-based emissions.

Many conservative Christians claim that they alone understand scripture. They assert some form of biblical literalism that trumps science, psychology, and global spirituality when these are in conflict. At the end of the day, these Christians uncritically subscribe to some version of the affirmation: "the Bible says it, I believe it, and that settles it!" Nevertheless, the external observer, unfamiliar with conservative and fundamentalist culture — including most seekers and a growing number of evangelical Christians - finds such literalist understandings of biblical authority problematic: conservative Christians oppose marriage equality and homosexuality based on a handful of opaque scriptures while accepting the realities of divorce and remarriage which are equally condemned in scripture; they fret about wedding cakes and bathrooms for transgender students, neither of which is mentioned in scripture, while extolling free-market capitalism and extreme vetting of refugees, despite the Bible's global condemnation of economic inequality and persecution of strangers.

At the end of the day, we must recognize that we all read the scriptures from certain perspectives, focusing on certain passages as definitive of divine revelation, while relegating others to irrelevance or ethical ambiguity. To take scriptural authority seriously, we need to read scripture holistically and, in the spirit of the Wesleyan quadrilateral, integrate our scripture reading with our best insights related to philosophy and theology, psychology and literature, tradition, and our own and our community's spiritual experience.

Progressive and emerging Christians have struggled with framing a theology of scriptural authority. Many, like myself, grew up in conservative churches, in which the Bible was unquestioned despite its textual and ethical inconsistencies. We found it necessary to question the faith of our childhoods when we were confronted by the realities of sexism, homophobia, injustice, intolerance, and parochialism perpetuated by literal readings of scripture. In my own case, for many years, after leaving the conservative Christian fold, I simply saw the Bible as simply a "good book," that is, a text containing a residue of spiritual and ethical counsel amid the chaff of myth, violence, and irrelevance. Like many others raised in conservative Christian households, who later jettisoned the faith perspectives of our childhood, I was in search of a way to understand biblical inspiration — or revelation — that could be integrated with the affirmation of the insights of science, medicine, religious pluralism, and human sexuality.

Seekers like myself recognized the unique impact of scripture in our own spiritual journeys. We regularly consulted scripture for spiritual guidance and edification, and in my case, we still preach regularly, write lectionary commentaries, and teach bible studies. In the process, we discovered a fallible yet inspirational text that was still important to us as a guide for understanding God's vision for our lives and the world.

Progressive Christians and recovering literalists, for the most part, now affirm that the wisdom and word of God enlightens all creation, including the religious insights of adherents of other faith traditions. An earthen vessel, fallible and finite, still scripture has changed our lives and this needs to be acknowledged in positive ways.

I have come to see scripture as a light for my journey. Its wisdom guides my ethical and spiritual path even though I don't assume scripture has all the answers to life's questions. I have also come to see the encounter with scripture — including its historical formation and the creation of the canon or authorized texts - as reflecting an interplay of divine inspiration and human creativity. Scripture is a part of God's ongoing call and response in history and individual human experience. As such, scripture is inspired, that is, God-breathed, providing us with insight for living. In the dynamic call and response of life, every aspect of the encounter with scripture reflects divine inspiration — the experience of the Hebraic and Jewish communities, mystics and prophets, the oral sharing from generation to generation, the words and descriptions of Jesus' ministry, the charismatic experiences of the early Christian community, the committing of tradition to paper, and the eventual compilation of scripture in terms of the texts that have shaped our faith.

The dynamic history of scriptural inspiration, formation, and reception also reflects the faithful experiences of fallible and finite humans trying to discern the wisdom of the Holy Mystery and Adventure we call God. The unique trajectory of scriptural inspiration and formation does not exclude the witness of the non-canonical Gnostic texts. We can find God's wisdom in the Gospel of Thomas just as we do in the Gospel of Mark or the Letter to the Galatians. Faithful Christians can critique calls to violence in scripture just as we critique the moral ambiguity of certain Quranic passages.

Our very reading of scripture also is inspired. God is still speaking within or beyond the words of scripture, providing inspiration, guidance, and challenge appropriate to our personal and political context. When we critique scriptural passages as scientifically irrelevant or recognize their ethical ambiguity and negative impact throughout history, we are not being unfaithful, but being "honest to God." We must challenge the words of scripture with the Word of Grace and Wisdom, recognizing both our fallibility and social location and God's wisdom moving in our lives and community.

The process of reading scripture faithfully also shapes the historical impact of revelation itself. Wrestling with scripture enables God to be more inspirational in our reading and reflections. Moreover, faithful reading of scripture embraces head, heart, and hands. In discovering the presence of God in scripture intellectually, we are inspired to experience the world in terms of God's compassion and share that compassion in our daily lives and political involvements. Reading scripture faithfully challenges our nation's attitudes about economics, immigration, diversity, sexuality, and the non-human world.

Scripture provides us with many fruitful possibilities for transformative living, and not a monolithic vision of life. We may discover that scripture gives us more than one "right" answer to many of life's most challenging questions. Yet, the consistent answers the Bible provides for human life are: love one another, welcome the stranger, ensure the well-being of the vulnerable, trust God's guidance, and know your life matters to God and that you can be God's partner in healing the world. The gospel — the good news of God's love for the world — comes through words, hands, hymns, hammers, picket signs, contemplation, and protest. The Bible comes to life when the words become flesh in our love for the world and our willingness to be part of God's realm of Shalom in its many and diverse manifestations.

Each of us has a "Bible within the Bible," the words that have been most transformative for us. From my perspective, we need a healthy and holistic biblical diet, encompassing a variety of emphases to promote healthy spirituality and mission within the church. As the saying goes, "you can find anything in the Bible." Still, your focus will determine your faith, spiritual practices, social ethics, attitudes toward science, pluralism, and earth care, and hope for the future.

Think about the scriptures that have nurtured your faith. Toward what do they orient you spiritually? Do they promote social as well as spiritual transformation? Do they open you to hear the cries of the poor and neglected? Do they enable you and your congregation to be both earthly-minded and heavenly good?

While I have lived with scripture for over sixty years, certain texts have uniquely shaped my spiritual journey. I share them to invite you to explore where scripture has transformed your life and inspired you to choose life in a death-filled world. My biblical faith has been shaped in good measure by living with four texts within the library of scripture: the book of Amos and its vision of the relationship between spirituality and social justice; Mark's focus on Jesus' healing ministry, encompassing body, mind, spirit, and social relationships; Acts of the Apostles' emphasis on mission and spirituality in a pluralistic context; and Philippians' connection of theological reflection and spiritual practices. Encountering these and other scriptures can change your life, and the Church Ahead must join theological reflection with biblical study, bringing heart, mind, soul, and hands to regular group and individual encounters with the Word and Wisdom of God.

THE BIBLE AS HEALING AND PROPHETIC

A healthy biblical diet includes the affirmation of prophetic challenge and personal and institutional healing. Ironically, many people, such as Franklin Graham and Jerry Falwell, Jr., who claim to take scripture literally disregard the prophetic challenges while focusing on the handful of passages relating to homosexuality and inventing out of thin air biblical warrants against the use of restrooms by transgendered persons. The biblical prophets served as intermediaries between God and humankind. Inspired by God to challenge the nation's values, the prophets were not fortune tellers nor did they give detailed predictions about the future. Rather, they starkly presented the consequences of social and political injustice. Directing their critiques against the wealthy and powerful, the prophets asserted that our actions enhance or diminish God's presence in the world. Turning from God can lead to national disaster not because God wishes to punish the people, but because in rejecting God's vision the nation cuts itself off from God's healing energy and inspiration. God hears the cries of the poor and laments the nation's injustice. What happens on earth matters to God; it shapes God's experience for better or worse, and it may open or block God's ability to guide and protect the nation.

Eight centuries before Jesus' birth, Amos, a shepherd from Tekoa, a small Judean village, was called by God to denounce the infidelity and injustice of the Northern Kingdom, Israel. Not unlike our time, the rich got richer and the poor became poorer. Despite the nation's apparent military security and economic prosperity, the end is near for the wealthy who "oppress the poor [and] crush the needy." (Amos 4:1) Their wealth is generated through greed and injustice. Their comfort is built on others' poverty. Economic and legal practices favor the wealthy at the expense of the working classes.

Injustice has a cost. In failing to hear the cries of the poor, the wealthy and powerful eventually become unable to experience God's presence. They perform complicated rituals with precision and make generous offerings to God only to discover that God hates and despises their festivals and takes no delight in their worship services. In speaking for God, the prophet proclaims:

> *Hear this, you that trample on the needy, and bring to ruin the poor of the land, saying, "When will the new moon be over so that we may sell grain; and the Sabbath, so that we may offer wheat for sale? We will make the ephah small and the shekel great, and practice deceit with false balances, buying the poor for silver and the needy for a pair of sandals, and selling the sweepings of the wheat".... The time is surely coming, says the Lord God, when I will send a famine on the land; not a famine of bread, or a thirst for water, but of hearing the words of the Lord. They shall wander from sea to sea, and from north to east; they shall run to and fro, seeking the word of the Lord, but they shall not find it.* (Amos 8:4-6, 11-12)

The wealthy and powerful assert their orthodoxy, sponsor elaborate services, and crackdown on deviants. Unaware of their impiety and greed — after all, it's just business and nothing personal — and the pain they are inflicting on the poor and the God of the vulnerable and poor, they forfeit the experience of God's grace. They are unable to hear the divine summons:

> *I hate, I despise your religious festivals; your assemblies are a stench to me. Even though you bring me burnt offerings and grain offerings, I will not accept them. Though you bring choice fellowship offerings, I will have no regard for them. Away with the noise of your songs! I will not listen to the music of your harps. But let justice roll on like a river, righteousness like a never-failing stream!* (Amos 5:21-24)

The words of Amos ring across the United States and the developed world today, especially in our churches. When Franklin Graham and other religious leaders proclaim that the Bible says nothing about immigration or care for vulnerable strangers, he turns the message of the prophets and Jesus on its head. Graham's words betray his own biblical illiteracy, to be generous, of passages that challenge the Hebraic people to welcome the stranger and give hospitality to the foreigner. Graham forgets that Jesus and his family were refugees. When preachers claim that God blesses unrestrained free-market capitalism and opposes universal health care, they turn their back on God's unique care for the poor and the prophetic denunciation of economic injustice and the gap between the wealthy and poor. We do well to remember the words of social gospel leader Walter Rauschenbusch that "It is possible to hold the orthodox doctrine on the devil and not recognize him when we meet him in a real estate office or at the stock exchange."

The jumbotrons and praise groups of megachurches may be the best money can buy, but they ring hollow if the poor are neglected and immigrants and refugees deported. When we privilege profits over prophets, we are reminded that what we do to the least of these, we do unto God. God is present in the marginalized, malnourished, forgotten, and vulnerable. God feels their hopelessness and pain, not as abstractions, but as God's own experience. Amos and his prophetic companions remind us that our calling in the micro and the macro is to "do something beautiful for God." Congregational singing of "Make America Great Again" is an anathema to the Divine One unless we first and foremost "let justice roll down like waters and righteousness like an ever-flowing stream," bathing the wealthy in compassion, the powerful in humility, the poor in prosperity, and the immigrant in hospitality.

The goal of the prophet is to heal the social order so that it reflects God's realm on earth as it is heaven. A prophet challenges the social order to embody God's vision of Shalom that brings healing to persons and institutions. In contrast to the prophets who spoke to religious and political leaders of their nation, Jesus and his first followers had no political power. Jesus spent the totality of his life under the thumb of the Roman empire. His spirit was free but his daily life was circumscribed by Roman power, whose machinations led to the cross. What appears to be a more individualistic and personal ethic, unrelated to politics, is in fact, Jesus' own prophetic message of healing and wholeness presented to a people without political power. Writ large, Jesus' message has political implications that can shape our economics, use of military force, and response to refugees, immigrants, and marginalized persons of all kinds.

The earliest written account of Jesus' ministry Mark's Gospel reflects Jesus' healing ministry, God's realm brought to earth in response to suffering humanity. Nearly half of the first ten chapters of Mark describes Jesus as a wandering healer, whose words, touch, and welcome bring healing of body, mind, spirit, and social standing. Healing, as Mark asserts, involves the whole person, our cells as well as our souls. Healing is this-worldly and has an eternal impact. Jesus' healings reflected his concern that people experience life in its fullness and this includes their place in society. Despite his political powerlessness, Jesus challenged the political and social ramifications of the Jewish religion. Just as Jesus' table fellowship reflected his vision of the all-embracing hospitality of God's realm, Jesus' healing ministry enabled outcasts, ostracized because of their health condition, to become full-fledged members of society once more. Healing embraced everyone and everything. Healed persons could once more take responsibility for their lives — they could go back to work, return to their families, walk proudly through city streets, and get married.

The progressive church has suffered due to its neglect of Jesus' healing ministry. We know we don't want to emulate the televangelists and their high-tech, theologically-unsound, and often manipulative approaches to healing. We rightly challenge the spurious connection of Jesus' nonjudgmental approach to healing with the success-oriented prosperity gospel, and its linear approach to health, wealth, and illness, which often blames the victim of illness or poverty for lack of faith, whether in the realm of physical well-being or economic success, and encourages a preferential option for the wealthy and successful in public policy. Our approach to healing, in contrast, must emphasize the interplay of call and response, grace and responsibility, and touch and technology. Holistic in nature, progressive visions of healing join prayer with protest. On the one hand, we recognize, with a growing body of scientific evidence, that prayer, spiritual practices, and faith can bring physical and spiritual restoration and promote overall well-being. This inspires us to initiate progressive, open-spirited healing services as well as to critically affirm the many emerging approaches to health and healing such as reiki healing touch, energy work, massage, yoga, Tai Chi, Qigong. Inspired by Jesus, our vision of healing is global in nature as it embraces high touch and high tech, meditation and medication, contemplation and chemotherapy, and prayer and Prozac, as my friend Dr. Dale Matthews advocates. On the other hand, healing transforms our social and political values. In the spirit of Jesus and the early Christian movement, and inspired by the prophets, we affirm the environmental, educational, and economic aspects of healing.

A holistic approach to healing includes ensuring a healthy environment and ecosystem on the planet as a totality as well as in Appalachian hollows, city streets, and seashore resorts; reducing gun violence; promoting economic and educational opportunity and equality; and providing universal systems of health promotion and care. A truly holistic vision of health challenges social values which promote polarization, marginalization, sexism, racism, homophobia, and xenophobia. In the spirit of the Kabbalistic affirmation, "when you save one soul, you save the world," our vision of health must transcend borders and embrace the immigrant and refugee while we seek ways to make agricultural implements out of military weapons. Healed people need a healed social order and healed planet to flourish and live out their vocation as God's beloved children.

I include Acts of the Apostles as a spiritual guide for our time because of its postmodern character, and a must-read for progressive-spirited Christians. "How," you might ask, "can a book written two thousand years ago be postmodern in spirit?" In a culture whose spirit is similar to our own, the early church emerged as a group of small communities seeking to be faithful in a pluralistic society whose values they did not share. The early Christian movement was spirit-filled. Decisions were made prayerfully. God's spirit animated their preaching and worship and drove them into the world to bring Christ's message to the whole earth. This spirit-led movement overcame the barriers of race, nationality, language, sexuality, and economics. Everyone was welcomed, despite differences in dialect and lifestyle. The early church sought to share all things common, overcoming the chasm between wealth and poverty and insuring that everyone had sufficient resources to live abundantly spirituality and domestically. Wealthier members chose to let go of their largesse so that others might move from survival mode to well-being.

Not unlike our time, the early Christian movement "made it up as it went along," creating rituals, communities, and theologies that were flexible and open-ended. Theology was "in the making" and new rituals were emerging. Jesus was central to the new movement's self-understanding, but no defining creeds or limiting authorities or rituals existed. The emerging Jesus movement's administration and order, and even its theology and leadership, were situational rather than abstract. The Spirit had a variety of manifestations and gifts specific to a variety of locations. While inability to deal with spiritual pluralism in the early Christian movement eventually led to conflict and the closing of the biblical canon, Spirit-led freedom and creativity animated the varieties of Christian experience and theology in the first decades of the movement. Orthopraxy, lived out in loving communities, trumped unbending orthodoxies whose purpose was as much to exclude as to welcome.

Today's emerging spiritual movements must be equally Spirit-led and flexible. They must be grounded, as Paul says in the Athenian marketplace of ideas, in the reality of God "in whom we live and move and have our being." (Acts 17:28) Committed to Christ, we need, like the early Christian movement, to affirm that wherever truth and healing are present, God is its source, whether these truths be found in other faiths, in scientific discovery, literary insights, or medical "miracles," acts of divine healing and power, and live with the hope of signs and wonders.

From the perspective of the wisdom of Acts of the Apostles, pluralism and postmodernism are not threats to a living Christianity, but rather the womb from which lively, transformative spirituality emerges. The postmodern quest for spiritual experience, and its suspicion of abstractions, invites us to experience God as a living reality, both personal and universal in its address to humankind and the non-human world, and revealed in many ways. Amid the tensions of theological and spiritual diversity, we can experience larger visions of ourselves and the world.

The journey through Acts takes us to Philippians and a first-century faith community whose existence depended on the leadership of a woman, Lydia. Philippians provides a transformational vision of spirit-centered theology and practice. Paul asserts that God is working in all things, leading them toward wholeness. God does not rule by power or domination. God's sovereignty is reflected in loving service and identification with humankind. God is with us not above us, inspiring us to empathy rather than apathy. God in Christ does not dominate but invites us to become partners in healing the world. Philippians' incarnational theology is inspired by a commitment to spiritual practices.

> *Rejoice in the Lord always; again I will say, Rejoice. Let your gentleness be known to everyone. The Lord is near. Do not worry about anything, but in everything by prayer and supplication with thanksgiving let your requests be made known to God. And the peace of God, which surpasses all understanding, will guard your hearts and your minds in Christ Jesus.*
>
> *Finally, beloved, whatever is true, whatever is honorable, whatever is just, whatever is pure, whatever is pleasing, whatever is commendable, if there is any excellence and if there is anything worthy of praise, think about these things. Keep on doing the things that you have learned and received and heard and seen in me, and the God of peace will be with you.* (Philippians 4:4-8)

Theology and spirituality are symbiotically related. Our spiritual experiences inspire theological reflection and theological reflection grounds our spiritual experiences in just and socially responsible actions.

Open-spirited understandings of scripture and theology breathe life into the church and welcome the wisdom of diverse spiritual perspectives. They invite our congregations to become lay seminaries, where wrestling with great ideas is nurtured, and life-changing practices emerge from serious study.

Grounded in solid theological and biblical reflection, our challenge in the final chapters of this text will be to explore more fully the role of worship, healing, prophetic social involvement, mysticism, and our attitudes toward time as essential to Christian mission in the church ahead.

SPIRITUALITY AND ACTION FOR THE CHURCH AHEAD

Spiritual Adventures. Today we need to go beyond literal understandings of the words of scripture to experience God's living word speaking through scripture and ourselves in our encounters with scripture. We need to move forward with creative and innovative approaches to reading and embodying the biblical witness. One imaginative way to encounter scripture is through the practice of *lectio divina* or holy reading, popularized by Benedictine spiritual guides. In this process of faith formation, which can be done individually or in small groups, we begin by focusing on a particular scripture, for example, the passage from Amos 8:4-6, 11-12, noted earlier in this chapter. In a twenty-first century version of holy reading, which can be applied to any literature and not just scripture, we employ the following steps:

1. A time of stillness and prayerful opening.
2. Prayer for guidance and wisdom.
3. Reading the scripture, followed by a time of silence.

4. Reading the scripture again, followed by a time of prayerful silence.
5. Listening for a word, song, image or phrase that emerges from the text.
6. Letting the word, phrase, song, or image soak in.
7. Asking God for insight into the meaning of what has surfaced.
8. Asking for God's help in embodying the text in your daily life.
9. Closing with prayer to embody the text.
10. Living the meaningful word, phrase, image, or song throughout the day.

Encountering the text imaginatively through *lectio divina* or imaginative prayer leads to comes personal and planetary transformation. Biblical thinking leads to Biblical acting in the city streets and the halls of Congress. The prophetic vision, embodied in lively spiritual practices, opens our hearts to the cries of the poor, the sighs of the neglected, the pain of the dying, and plight of the unwelcome as we seek God's Shalom for just such a time as this, embodied by just such a people as us.

Contemplative Action. The Bible inspires a holistic spirituality in which the word is made flesh in community involvement. The Bible challenges us to join right belief with right action on the personal and community levels. *If your congregation does not currently offer Bible studies, you might consider offering some of the following to encourage active spirituality: 1) A seminar on the theme of "Introduction to the Bible," 2) A six-week study on Acts of the Apostles, inviting participants to reflect on the characteristics of a lively spirit-centered, dynamically mission-oriented church, 3) A six-week study comparing the book of Amos with Jesus' Sermon on the Mount (Matthew, Chapters 5-7) to orient the community to the integration of faith and social change.*

CHAPTER TEN

SPIRIT SIGHTINGS

Moses was keeping the flock of his father-in-law Jethro, the priest of Midian; he led his flock beyond the wilderness, and came to Horeb, the mountain of God. There the angel of the Lord appeared to him in a flame of fire out of a bush; he looked, and the bush was blazing, yet it was not consumed. Then Moses said, "I must turn aside and look at this great sight, and see why the bush is not burned up." (Exodus 3:1)

One of my favorite rabbinical stories involves Moses and the burning bush. As this ancient story goes, Moses is on his way to work tending his father-in-law's flocks. Raised in wealth and groomed for power, Moses is now a fugitive in the wilderness, working long hours and trying to raise a family. His dreams of making a difference for his people have been shattered by the drudgery of shepherding. Moses is astounded when without warning, he sees a bush that is burning, but not consumed by the flames. He almost faints when he hears a voice from the bush, commanding him to take off his shoes for he is standing on holy ground. In the ongoing dialogue, between Moses and divinity hidden in a bush, Moses discovers his vocation.

Not content with literal interpretations of Moses' encounter with God, according to legend, the rabbis debate the question, "Why was the bush burning but not consumed by the flames?" They go around and round, coming up with erudite solutions to the riddle, until one rabbi asserts, "The bush was burning but not consumed so that one day, as he walked by, Moses would finally notice it!"

For many days as he commuted to work, Moses passed by the bush and saw nothing of consequence. But, one day, his eyes were opened. He paused long enough to see the spectacle and discover that God had been with him all along, waiting for him to notice.

Spirit-sightings can be seismic in nature. They can turn your world upside down. Jacob dreams of a ladder of angels, ascending from earth to heaven, and exclaims "God is in this place, and I did not know it." Daydreaming about her upcoming nuptials, Mary of Nazareth is visited by an angel, inquiring if she is willing to be the mother of God's Savior and Healer. Saul of Tarsus is struck down by a shimmering light, revealing the Risen Jesus, while on his way to arrest followers of the Risen One. He receives a new name, a new life, and a new direction.

Most spirit-sightings are ordinary and every day in nature. There is no dramatic piercing of the veil between heaven and earth. No angelic visitation. But, in a holy moment, we realize that we are in a "thin place," and that whole earth, including us, is filled with God's glory. We may never hear an audible voice of God, but we may, like John Wesley, experience a "strangely warmed" heart or a counsel from a mentor that guides us, like Queen Esther, toward our vocation for "just such a time as this." God's call often happens within the everyday events of life, suddenly illuminating them for what they are, revelations of the One in whom we live and move and have our being. We still chop wood and carry water as the Buddhist sages assert, but now every task is chock-full with holiness.

As I write these words, I recall a recent Ash Wednesday Worship Service at South Congregational Church and our congregation's six-week experiment in adventurous spiritual practices. Today, there is a growing interest in spiritual practices, personal and corporate rituals done daily as ways to experience God's presence and calling more clearly. In the Lenten season, our spiritual practices may be described in terms of pruning a fruit tree, eliminating branches that are dead and get in the way of our spiritual growth. As an apple farmer once told me, "I prune my trees to let the sun shine in." Regardless of our political leaders' response to global climate change, we need to exceed the expectations of the Paris Accords in our daily lives and urge our local municipalities and national government to do so as well. We need to simplify our lives so our planet can simply live! We need to de-clutter our homes and also our spiritual lives and domestic lifestyles.

Progressive and socially-active Christians are recognizing that it is essential to balance contemplation and action to enlighten our protests and avoid demonizing our opponents. When we, in the spirit of William Blake and Aldous Huxley, cleanse the doors of perception, we see reality as infinite and God-breathed.

Progressive and emerging Christians — culturally creative Christians — affirm a variety of spiritual practices, suited to age, intellectual interest, personality type, ethnicity, previous religious experience, and congregational community. Moreover, we recognize that persons can benefit from using positions from a variety of denominational and religious traditions. We affirm that wherever truth and healing are found, God is its source, whether we discover it at a Pentecostal prayer service, Zen monastery, Benedictine retreat house, Quaker meeting, or quietly meditating in our living room. The variety of spiritual practices give us, as Rumi asserts, a hundred ways to kneel and kiss the earth in gratitude for God's blessings.

Many persons today are "global" or "inter-spiritual" in their religious practices. They creatively and fluidly synthesize wisdom and experiences from a variety of faith traditions in light of their Christian faith. This should not be discouraged, provided our churches and their leaders enable congregants to connect these practices with a holistic vision of the way of Jesus, joining contemplation and action in embracing our role as God's companions in healing the world.

In the following paragraphs, I chart one holistic path toward community spiritual transformation, grounded in the seasons of the Christian year. The seasons of the Christian year join the way of Jesus with the way of the earth, articulated by the earth-oriented spiritual traditions. They sanctify time and give meaning to space. Living the seasons of the Christian year provides a balanced diet of action and contemplation and of focus on the various aspects of human personality and vocation. The practices I list are evocative and not prescriptive. You may even join them with earth-based pagan rituals of the seasons — solstice and equinox — to ground your spirituality in natural as well as liturgical rhythms as well as to discover the transformative resources of an oft-maligned spiritual tradition. Let them inspire you to explore other practices, that resonate with your current spiritual adventures.

The Encircling Year

The circle of the Christian year begins right after Thanksgiving with *Advent,* the season of waiting and hope in what is unseen. *Advent* is a time for pregnancy and birthing in which we are challenged to midwife the coming of God's realm in our lives and in the world. We live in a broken world which calls us to be God's companions in healing the Earth.

A spirituality of Advent, the first season of the Christian year, involves visualizing the healing of the Earth. As midwives of a new world order, we need to make room for God's birth in the world. Accordingly, we need to make space for God's birth within us through moments in which we "pause" to "be still" in God's presence. Then, we need to imagine, in the spirit of John Lennon's hymn, God's dream for our world as a prelude to becoming ambassadors for a world in which:

> *they shall beat their swords into plowshares,*
> *and their spears into pruning hooks;*
> *nation shall not lift up sword against nation,*
> **neither shall they learn war any more.** (Isaiah 2:5)

Moreover, we are challenged to visualize what the world and our nation would be like if we:

> *let justice roll down like waters, and righteousness like an ever-flowing stream.* (Amos 5:24)

From contemplation and visualization, we can move toward actions that bring peace and justice, first, in our families and churches and, then, our communities and nation where pregnancy leads to a politics of protection for the vulnerable children and expectant mothers.

The Christmas Season is the season of light amid the darkness. These days, we must search for light wherever it can be found. The light of Christmas points to the presence of Christ amid the chaos of world history and our own lives. This light cannot be quenched, but illumines our path when it is most needed. In the fullness of time, Jesus is born among the powerless and oppressed. Shortly after his birth, his family must flee to Egypt seeking asylum to avoid certain death. Jesus' parents like millions of refugees today are simply looking for a safe place to raise their child. Fearful of new creation, the Herod-like political leaders want to destroy anything that would stand in the way of profit and power. They prefer death to life and profit to prophetic witness. They believe that life and creativity must be stamped out to preserve the old order's ability to define reality. In Christmas, we embrace the spirituality of Mother Teresa who sought to experience God in God's most distressing disguises and look for innovation and imagination wherever it is hidden and bring it forth.

A spirituality of Christmas looks for light in life's most unexpected places. Our meditations begin with imagining a divine light flowing in us with every breath until we are filled with God's enlivening and enlightening radiance. From this enlightened moment, we open our senses to God's light in everyone we meet. With the Quakers, we look for something of God in the stranger and the opponent. Aware of our own inner light, we begin to experience the inner light in others. Jesus says, "You are the light of the world…let your light shine." So let this divine light radiate from us to bring truth and healing to every place of disease and chaos whether in the White House, the halls of Congress, city streets, or rural hamlets. As John's Gospel proclaims, the true light present in Jesus enlightens all creation and every person. Like the innkeeper in Bethlehem, we cultivate practices of hospitality that join individual and corporate compassion.

The Season of Epiphany is the season of the magi, spiritual leaders and astrologers from a faraway land who follow a star to the Christ-child. Epiphany is also a season of enlightenment in which we embrace the light in others as well as ourselves. During the season of epiphany, we look for holiness in the wisdom of other cultures and discover spiritual common ground with persons of other faiths and with persons of diverse theological and political perspectives within our own faith tradition.

During Epiphany, we sojourn to the East and the West through practicing "walking prayer." Abraham Joshua Heschel describes his experience marching with Martin Luther King in Selma, "it felt like my legs were praying." As you walk, breathe slowly and prayerfully, letting your movement push you forward toward God's realm.

Breath prayer is an essential practice in most religious traditions. Relax in God's presence: then begin to breathe slowly and gently imaging God's Spirit entering you with every breath. Experience your exhaling joining you with all creation in one vast Breath of Life.

As part of your Epiphany spiritual formation, take time to learn about another religious tradition. Many congregations invite a Muslim, Hindu, Jewish, or Buddhist spiritual leader to share about their faith. Your congregation might also study the indigenous religions of the Americas and Africa as well as earth-based faiths in search of common ground. In these times, let your Epiphany spirituality inspire you to stand with persons, even in North America, who are persecuted because of their faith tradition. You may choose to boldly spend an afternoon watching Christian televangelists or programs on Fox News to gain familiarity — and perhaps sympathy- with viewpoints quite different than your own.

The Lenten Season is the time of pruning, of eliminating all that clutters our spiritual, relational, professional, and communal lives. Lent is the time of examination, a time in which we look in the mirror of our lives and eliminate everything, even certain "good things" that stand between us and our calling as God's companions in bringing beauty and healing to this good Earth.

Lent reminds us of Jesus' vision of our relationship with God in terms of vines and branches. Connected with God, we bear fruit in great abundance. Disconnected, our spirits wither and die. We prune the unnecessary branches so that God's light can shine in and through us and so that we can bear fruits of healing and wholeness.

During Lent, we need to recover the practice of Examen, or examination of conscience. In the Examen, we look at our lives daily, reflecting on our relationship with God. We take time to give thanks for God's blessings in our life and to review the day we've just spent, considering those moments when we drew near to God and when we turned away for God's vision for our lives.

Today, our practice of the Examen must be global as well as individual. We need to ask ourselves: Where have we contributed to the well-being of the planet and where we have turned away in our lifestyle from creative and life-supporting Earth-care? Our questions need to give birth to actions that promote the healing of the planet. We need to make a commitment to live more simply so that others — our human and non-human companions — may simply live.

Holy Week invites us to share in the suffering of the world. God is the fellow sufferer who understands and in seeking to follow God's way, we need to be attentive to suffering in our communities, nation, and the planet. God feels our pain and the pain of every creature. Faithfulness to God challenges us to move from apathy to empathy.

During Holy Week, we can experience the sacred heart of Jesus through praying the headlines. Prayerfully embrace the pain and beauty of life and the wonder of creation. Look for God in all God's distressing disguises. Let our prayers take wings in ways that respond to the pain we view in the headlines.

A few years ago we began what may become a Holy Week tradition at the Cape Cod congregation where I serve as pastor. We walked the "stations of the cross" on the beach as a sign of our solidarity with the non-human world and our willingness to bring healing to the pain of creation. Our consumption contributes not only to the pain of our fellow humans but to the non-human world. We have much to repent as begin to love the Creator by loving the creation. In the future, we may also sponsor a second stations of the cross in Hyannis to spotlight homelessness and poverty.

    The Easter Season is countercultural in body and spirit. Poet-activist Wendell Berry challenges us to "practice resurrection." We truly live in a world in which suffering and uncertainty reign. It is easy to lose hope when the forces of death are aligned against the values we hold dear. The cross symbolizes death in all its forms. Holy Saturday reminds us that the future is open and uncertain. Jesus' first disciples had no expectation of a resurrection. Jesus was dead and with his death, all hope was lost for them. Yet, on Easter morning, Jesus rises and they can live again. Christ is alive and so are they; an empty tomb gives way to an open future.

    In Easter, we challenge death-filled living, whether perpetuated by governments, institutions, or individuals. Deathful behaviors and attitudes deaden the spirit and diminish hope. Resurrection living brings hope to hopeless situations and enables us to rise from the ashes to experience everlasting life amid all of life's ambiguities. As we practice resurrection, we proclaim that love is stronger than fear and life more resilient than death.

    It is time to sing "Alleluia" and claim new life. It is time to sing hymns of new creation and celebrate the fecundity of the Earth. During Easter, look for signs of life and bring them forth, first, through prayerful petitions and intercessions and then protest and response to all that threatens life. In the Easter season, challenge death in all its forms, remembering that when we save one soul, we save the world.

    The Season of Pentecost is the season of giftedness, a time to discover our vocations as individuals and communities. During Pentecost, reflect regularly on the coming of the Spirit, described in Acts 2 along with Paul's reflection spiritual gifts, found in I Corinthians 12. Make a commitment not only to nurture your own spiritual gifts but to create an environment of giftedness in your relationships and political involvement. Pentecost involves bringing hope to the children. The church's primary role is to nurture dreams, and dreams are the stuff of childhood. Pentecost awakens limitless possibilities in the child in us and the children in our midst. Pentecost inspires us to place the future of children, especially neglected and impoverished children, as central to our own well-being. In the Pentecost, the mission of the church is to move from self-interest to world loyalty and from survival to sacrificial service.

During Pentecost, make a commitment to explore the gifts emerging in your life and communities for just such a time as this. All of us have many vocations, and many gifts. Each moment has a vocation. Let your daily prayer be motivated by Jesus' counsel to "ask, seek, and knock." Pray boldly and then open to new possibilities emerging for yourself and your communities.

Every person has a vocation. In pondering our own vocations, we are led to support the vocations of our neighbors — enabling them by our actions and political commitments — to achieve their divinely-inspired callings. Make a commitment to support the growth of children in your church, community, nation, and across the globe.

Creation Season. During the second half of Pentecost, many congregations are beginning to focus on the Season of Creation. They recognize that many of us have been so heavenly minded that we have forgotten the Earth that gives us life. As Pope Francis asserts, we have made the earth a garbage dump through our consumerism. We have focused on immediate profits rather than the survival of endangered species and generations to come.

During the Creation Season, we are challenged to listen and see. On the one hand, we need to train our senses to hear the cries of creation. Begin by listening to song birds in your neighborhood. Purchase a CD on the song of the humpbacked whale or the hymns of dolphins speaking to one another.

As you sojourn throughout the day, open your senses to beauty. Take a beauty break, as theologian and spiritual guide Patricia Adams

Farmer counsels. Bathe your eyes in beauty. Take time to be amazed at the wonders of life. Pray with your eyes open, looking for God's presence in every encounter.

Creation season invites congregations to care for the immediate environment — to do park and beach cleanup projects, plant trees, plant milkweed plants for butterflies. But beyond the neighborhood, creation season challenges us to reduce our carbon footprint and challenge our national leaders to put the planet ahead of profits. This may involve letter writing and calls to congressional leaders or public protests of environmentally destructive political policies.

SPIRITUALITY AND ACTION FOR THE CHURCH AHEAD

Spiritual Adventures. This chapter has highlighted several spiritual practices to which I add two simple walking prayers.

In the spirit of the First Americans, we can as we walk, repeat over and over again: "With beauty all around me I walk."

Following the sages of Celtic Christianity, we can as we walk, repeat step by step a prayer attributed to St. Patrick:

> Christ with me, Christ before me, Christ behind me, Christ in me, Christ beneath me, Christ above me, Christ on my right, Christ on my left, Christ when I lie down, Christ when I sit down, Christ in the heart of everyone who thinks of me, Christ in the mouth of everyone who speaks of me, Christ in the eye that sees me, Christ in the ear that hears me. In our walking, we will discover Christ as our companion, Spirit as our inspiration, and Divine Parent as our protection.

These same prayers can be practiced while seated by simply experiencing the beauty of life around you, recognizing you are always surrounded by God's grace as you repeat these prayers.

Contemplative Actions. In our increasingly busy world in which there is little time for silence and reflection, consider the following practices to nurture sacred time: *You might involve a small group in your church to plan special activities for each of the seasons of the Chris-*

tian year. What might you focus on in prayer and action to embody the holy gifts of each season? For example, in Creation Season, your congregation might make a commitment to participate in a neighborhood cleanup, inviting the partnership of neighbors. You might also have a seminar on ways to live more simply to support the well-being of the planet. Many people go on the carbon fast during Lent, using fewer fossil fuels, to promote planetary well-being. In the Epiphany season, you might reach out to a family or religious group of another ethnicity or culture, inviting them to share a meal and faith stories.

CHAPTER ELEVEN

WORSHIP INSPIRING WONDER

*Praise the L*ORD*! Praise God in his sanctuary; praise God in his mighty firmament!*
Praise God for God's mighty deeds; praise him
  according to his surpassing greatness!
Praise God's with trumpet sound; praise God with lute and harp!
Praise God with tambourine and dance;
  praise God with strings and pipe!
Praise God with clanging cymbals;
  praise God with loud clashing cymbals!
Let everything that breathes praise the Lord! Praise the Lord!
(Psalm 150)

The great Jewish theologian and spiritual leader Abraham Joshua Heschel asserted that radical amazement and a sense of wonder are at the heart of religious experience. If you can't be amazed at the heavens above, the earth teeming with flora and fauna, and the gifts of the sea, you are hardly religious, the Jewish theologian and mystic believed.

Alfred North Whitehead once noted that religion is what a person does with her or his solitariness. We all need times to be alone, communicating with God, reflecting on our lives, and listening to our deepest yearnings. Yet, we are also part of a dynamic fabric of relationships which remind us that our religious lives are also deeply communal.

We can pause regularly for meditation and devotional reading. Our spirits are transformed as we walk along the beach or hike in the woods. In the still of the night, we hear the voice of God calling to us in questions and dreams. We can even pause on a busy street to see holiness in the faces of busy passersby. But, we also gather as faith communities for mutual affirmation, praise, song, and celebration. We hear the scriptures addressed to us as persons in community. We gather as families of faith, sharing each other's joys and sorrows. Worship also inspires wonder. Our hymns elevate our spirits and place us on higher ground. Reflections on scripture give us guidance for navigating the complexities of life. The intimacy of persons who worship beside one another year after year creates circles of love that extend far beyond our families to embrace the whole earth. In worship, we learn we are connected with people we may never meet — homeless persons in the inner city, victims of gun violence, and hungry children in Somalia and Appalachia. Worship opens our hearts to both the pain and joy of the world.

WORSHIP AS MISSION

Everything a congregation does is mission and this includes our times of worship. While worship is intrinsically valuable in its nurture of our spirits — its comfort, consolation, inspiration and insight shape us as persons — worship also drives us, like the early Christian movement on Pentecost, out into the streets to be God's partners in healing the earth. Holistic worship is ancient and future, and it is also *now* — embedded in and moving forward from this holy moment into a world of wonder, chaos, and complexity. The point of dedicated prayer is to make all life a prayer. As Abraham Joshua Heschel described marching with Martin Luther King in Selma, "it felt like my legs were praying." The point of worship is also so that all life becomes worshipful, all life holy, reverential, and amazing. The perspective and friendship gained in worship translate to stature and hospitality in our daily lives. Worship breaks down the walls that separate humankind into friends and enemies, neighbors and strangers, progressives and conservatives, Democrats and Republicans. We discover that we are all God's beloved children, worthy of love, affirmation, and welcome.

Holistic worship joins body, mind, and spirit, and embraces the breadth of cultures, styles, and media, appropriate to any given community. There are times worship needs to comfort and console. But, other times, we need, as Annie Dillard counsels, to put on safety helmets and lash ourselves to our pews as the challenges of worship turn our world upside down and challenge our ways of life.

With Amos the shepherd-prophet from Tekoa, progressive and emerging worship breaks down the walls between sanctuary and street corner. As Amos proclaimed, worship without justice-seeking leads to a famine in hearing the word of God. Worship without concern for the vulnerable, both human and non-human, degenerates into a social club. When America or Nation First religious leaders say Christianity has nothing to do with issues of hospitality to immigrants and refugees, their bloviations drown the word and wisdom of God among those who trust his counsel. This unbiblical vision deadens our spirits and dims our vision, and rendering our worship a social club, pity party of whining Christians, and silo of apathy and suspicion. As Amos warns:

> *The time is surely coming, says the Lord God, when I will send a famine on the land; not a famine of bread, or a thirst for water, but of hearing the words of the Lord.*
> *They shall wander from sea to sea, and from north to east; they shall run to and fro, seeking the word of the Lord, but they shall not find it.* (Amos 8:11-12)

There is nothing wrong with beautiful sanctuaries and attractive church buildings.

Brick and mortar are also holy, and our sanctuaries can be "thin places" where we experience divine inspiration. Lively music and insightful preaching changes lives and inspires action. Fellowship provides support from generation to generation. But, unless our worship reflects the vision of a "house of prayer for all people," (Isaiah 56:7) our words will be hollow and our hymns flat. While God is not a Democrat or Republican or progressive or conservative, our worship destroys our spirits, and creates a chasm between faith communities and the world, if we fail to hear the cries of the poor and respond individually and politically to create economies of grace and structures of justice. As Amos' contemporary, the prophet Micah affirms:

> *With what shall I come before the Lord, and bow myself before God on high? Shall I come before him with burnt offerings, with calves a year old? Will the Lord be pleased with thousands of rams, with ten thousands of rivers of oil? Shall I give my firstborn for my transgression, the fruit of my body for the sin of my soul?"*
>
> *He has told you, O mortal, what is good; and what does the Lord require of you but to do justice, and to love kindness, and to walk humbly with your God?* (Micah 8:6-8)

Jumbotrons and praise bands add nothing to worship unless our worship inspires large-heartedness and care for the lonely, forgotten, and unfamiliar in our midst. Worship inspires faith not fear, and love not isolation.

Alive and Messy Worship

Today, we hear the phrase "messy church" as a way of encouraging intergenerational, lively, and spontaneous worship. The messiness of worship also applies to our connection with the world. When we pray, we take time to give thanks for the wonders of creation and the daily blessings of health, family, and work; we also set aside time to utter words of petition and intercession for our own trials and tribulations and the pain of the world. Worship is messy, because large-souled worship awakens us to pain as well as wonder, to injustice as well as blessing, to violence as well as calm. Even though our worship services may bound on the homogenous in terms of ethnicity and economics, we can invite pluralism and diversity into our worship with songs from across the globe, affirmation of global worship styles, and prayers for persons across the globe and our nation. We can be a "village church with a global perspective," as I describe our Cape Cod church. We can also be an urban church that opens its doors to the lost and the lonely. Our commitment to local spirituality can become an open door to welcome the planet in all its wonder and pain. We can become a place, as a Washington DC church marquee affirmed, "where all are pilgrims but none are strangers."

In our increasingly pluralistic world in which there are a growing number of "nones" and "dones" as well as self-described "spiritual but not religious" persons, service to the larger community must become essential in our congregations' worship and faith formation. Churches that care for the people of their immediate neighborhood as well as far ranging communities must be willing to welcome outsiders to participate in rituals of faith such as weddings, memorial services and funerals, as well as services responding to national or global crises such as the mass murders at Las Vegas and Sutherland Springs, the hurricanes in Texas, Florida, and Puerto Rico, forest fires in California, and the racist marchers in Charlottesville. Pastors must be willing to become interfaith and secular chaplains creatively crafting worship services and being available as spiritual companions to persons who will never regularly attend their congregations. With John Wesley, we must remember that our parish is the world. The interplay of local and global in worship and mission has become more essential for congregations in this time of pandemic, which challenges congregations to explore new and creative forms of worship that embrace vulnerable persons in our community. These changes may lead to more instrumental music and less singing and hands folded in welcome rather than hugs during passing the peace. Innovative forms of worship may be required to be faithful to God and the wellbeing of our neighbors.

ANCIENT, FUTURE, NOW

Holistic and life-transforming worship can emerge from a variety of styles. Eclectic in spirit and reflecting the nature of a community in its interaction with larger communities, vital and spirit-centered worship can involve practices as diverse as:

- Taizé chants and silence
- Gospel hymns and synthesizers
- Praise songs and pensive silence
- Bach, the Beatles, and U-2
- Poetry and psalms

- Bluegrass and Beethoven
- Ancient hymns and post-modern prose
- Body prayer and stillness
- Laying on of hands and anointing
- Deep prayer and intellectual messages
- Short affirmations and words from the mystics
- Films and light shows
- Dance and body prayer
- Loud crashing symbols and deep stillness
- Artists and academics
- Social activism and congregational care
- Prophetic restlessness and mystic calm
- Multi-sensory and silent focus

There are many paths to wholeness in worship. All share in affirming the unique identity and spirit of a community, while leaning toward new possibilities. All spiral forth from the center of a community's practices to embrace larger and larger circles of care. Dynamic worship recognizes that the "center is everywhere" — God is here in this place. It also affirms that "there is no other" — we are intimately connected with all creation. Worship that has stature of size awakens us to diversity, contrast, multiple intelligences and media, in the context of a community's unique style of worship. Still, regardless of where a congregation is in its worship style, openness to new forms of worship, congruent with the community's spiritual identity is essential for ongoing growth and vitality.

Worship is always lived in the "now," although healthy worship recognizes its connectedness with all times and places, but most especially with the challenge of this present time. It is "ancient" in its openness to the wisdom of the past, the living faith of past generations. It is "future" in its willingness to look beyond tradition and familiarity to discern God's new possibilities. It is centered in a community, but reaches out in relatedness to the world. In the interdependent nature of life, we celebrate communion with Syrian refugees and Russian Orthodox communities. We share bread and wine with members of inner-city storefront churches, Appalachian Pentecostals, high church Anglicans, and South American base communities. Everyone is gathered around the table of God's blessing and "everyone" takes us beyond Christianity to affirm our solidarity with all humanity and the non-human world.

Vital worship doesn't erect walls but opens doors to God's Spirit. It doesn't whine about the "war" on Christmas, but brings the cosmic Christ to everyday life. It doesn't berate seekers, agnostics, and adherents of other faiths, but inspires communities of open-hearted hospitality.

Worship inspires wonder, gratitude, amazement, appreciation, and care. Christ is alive and affirms and transcends our rituals and worship styles, inviting us to adventurous creativity and faithfulness. God is on the journey with us, inspiring us to prayer, praise, and prophetic action.

Spirituality and Action for the Church Ahead

Spiritual Adventures. If you are a part of a worshipping community, let your community membership call you to prayer. Throughout the week, take time to pray for your worship leaders and community members. Visualize the worship space and persons in attendance. You may even pray for persons in the church directory, one page at a time, over the next several days. Pray that your congregation, like the early Pentecost communities, be open to novel and creative movements of God's Spirit in the integration of worship and mission. Pray for the strangers who haven't yet entered your worship space, and pray that all who enter will find a home. Pray that when unexpected visitors enter — especially the lost and lonely, the vulnerable and voiceless — that you welcome them with large and loving hearts. Pray about your congregation's mission to the "nones," "dones," and "spiritual but not religious" in your community as well as those who fear deportation or are at risk because of their citizenship status.

Contemplative Action. Worship is dynamic, global, and multi-sensory. To respond to our deepest needs as well as the needs of seekers, your congregation may choose to consider the following contemplative actions: *1) The formation of seasonal worshipping committees, whose task is to explore innovative forms of worship, promoting personal spirituality and congregational action, appropriate to the particular seasons of the church year; 2) Inviting youth and children to have roles in leading worship and making the service more intergenerational in spirit; 3) Sponsoring short seminars following worship to explore the scriptural themes high-lighted in the sermon and service; and 4) greater commitment to online worship and study to respond to the ongoing needs of housebound and vulnerable persons and expand congregational worship beyond the sanctuary.*

CHAPTER TWELVE

HEALING HANDS OF JESUS

Now there was a woman who had been suffering from hemorrhages for twelve years. She had endured much under many physicians, and had spent all that she had; and she was no better, but rather grew worse. She had heard about Jesus, and came up behind him in the crowd and touched his cloak, for she said, "If I but touch his clothes, I will be made well." Immediately her hemorrhage stopped; and she felt in her body that she was healed of her disease. Immediately aware that power had gone forth from him, Jesus turned about in the crowd and said, "Who touched my clothes?" And his disciples said to him, "You see the crowd pressing in on you; how can you say, 'Who touched me?'" He looked all around to see who had done it. But the woman, knowing what had happened to her, came in fear and trembling, fell down before him, and told him the whole truth. He said to her, "Daughter, your faith has made you well; go in peace, and be healed of your disease." (Mark 5:25-33)

The quest for healing in our time inspires me to elaborate on the discussion of healing in Mark's Gospel, found earlier in this text. Jesus' mission, then and now, involves the healing of persons, relationships, and nations. Jesus had no access to halls of government and the centers of wealth, nor did he have the benefits of health insurance and modern medicine, Jesus sought a world in which God's vision would come "on earth as it is heaven." Jesus saw health as multi-dimensional and that includes communities as well as persons.

Jesus' first public address affirmed on the holistic vision of the prophet Isaiah:

The Spirit of the Lord is upon me, because he has anointed me to bring good news to the poor. He has sent me to proclaim release to the captives and recovery of sight to the blind, to let the oppressed go free, to proclaim the year of the Lord's favor. (Luke 4:18-19)

According to Luke, Jesus' mission statement involved the healing of persons and the social order. It embraced the ordinary as well as the miraculous. Followers of Jesus are challenged to join his quest for Shalom, the peaceful and healthy ordering of society and human life.

The Gospel of John elaborates on Luke's mission statement: "I came that they might have life and have it abundantly." (John 10:10) Jesus' mission is to heal, transform, connect, and inspire, and not punish, judge, alienate, or oppress. God is out to love you, not to punish or shame you.

The gospels proclaim that healing of persons was at the heart of Jesus' mission. But, Jesus recognized that the healing of bodies is joined with the healing of spirits, relationships, and social status. In a society in which religious beliefs sanctioned the ostracism of persons with certain health ailments, Jesus' hospitality embraced everyone. Jesus healed cells, souls, and society. Jesus didn't blame the victim, but restored her or him to full participation in the social and religious order as a sign of God's all-embracing realm of Shalom.

THE HEALING LANDSCAPE OF THE 21ST CENTURY

Today, health and healing are central to the spiritual journey of millions of North Americans. Despite the advances in medical care, physicians and patients alike have come to realize that health involves the whole person — body, mind, spirit, emotions, relationships, workplace, education, economics, housing, and accessibility to health care. The role of spirituality in health and well-being is now supported by scientific studies, which note that meditation promotes overall health and stress reduction, faith has a role in recovery from illness, and persons who are active in religious communities are typically healthier and live longer than those who do not participate in houses of worship. Medical studies also suggest that intercessory prayer may be a factor in recovery from illness.

In a holistic and interdependent universe, our prayers create a field of positive energy around those for whom we pray. Our prayers transform our attitudes and create a bond with those for whom we pray, creating an energetic connection that can transform cells as well as souls.

Scientists and physicians as well as laypeople affirm the value of alternative health care practices such as yoga, Tai Chi, reiki, qigong, and massage in promoting spiritual and emotional calm and insight as well as physical well-being. Accordingly, the church today needs to be a laboratory for holistic prayer and healing. Church Ahead seeks to integrate Jesus' healing ministry and the power of prayer and contemplative practices with the growing interest in alternative medical practices.

The church of the future is called to be, in the language of Martin Luther King, a headlight and not a taillight in responding to the quest for healing and the integration of faith and alternative medicine. Inspired by the ministry of Jesus, understood in the context of today's holistic medicine and theology, the church's calling is to be a house of prayer and healing for all people: a place to welcome and accept persons seeking healing and wholeness of body, mind, spirit, and relationships. The congregation I pastor, South Congregational Church, United Church of Christ, on Cape Cod sponsors a reiki healing group, regular healing prayer services, and occasional Christianity and yoga classes. Typical of today's growing inter-spiritual, hybrid, or global spirituality movements, many of our members practice yoga, qigong, reiki, Tai Chi, along with Christian spiritual practices. Our mission is to see these various healing practices as reflections of Jesus' vision of abundant life as we affirm that wherever healing occurs, God is its source.

HEALING AS MISSION AND SOCIAL TRANSFORMATION

Open-spirited Christianity has a lot of work to do if seekers are to find spiritual homes and healing sites in our congregations.

Studies indicate that seekers and persons outside the church, especially younger persons, see the church as anti-science, anti-woman, anti-GLBTQ, and anti-medicine. What they do know about Christianity and health involves, on the one hand, strident opposition to women's reproductive rights, and on the other, flamboyant prosperity gospel preachers and television faith healers. While affirmative spirituality and healing prayer have an essential place in holistic Christianity, seekers within and outside the church often view these movements as blessing materialism and consumption as Christian values and citing peoples' lack of faith as the reason for their poverty or ill-health. Further, prosperity gospel teachers and televangelists have been among the staunchest advocates of political policies that favor the wealthy, deny health care access to the poorest Americans, and condemn the LGBT community as deviant and sinful. Jesus, however, offers another healing path — a path that welcomes the seeker and broken-spirited, a path that embraces persons regardless of their social standing, sexuality, health condition, and marital status.

Jesus' Healing Ministry Today

Jesus' healing ministry is as current as today's research on the role of spirituality in health and well-being. While we cannot replicate Jesus' healing ministry in the context of Western technological medicine and its diagnostic, surgical, and pharmaceutical methodologies, Jesus' healing ministry joins high touch and compassionate hospitality with the high tech to which we have become accustomed.

Jesus touched and listened. He healed persons by the transfer of healing energy. He also healed persons by inspiring faith (the placebo effect), forgiveness (guilt can damage our cells as well as our souls), hospitality and acceptance, listening and welcoming. Jesus' ministry was grounded in seeing persons' lives as dynamically interdependent. Moving within all things was God's gentle providence, aiming at healing, wholeness, and abundant life.

Jesus' approach to healing and wholeness embraces the individual and social dimensions of healing and asserts that the healing of persons is intimately related to planetary healing. In speaking of the impact of environment and social context on overall well-being, social gospel preacher Walter Rauschenbusch noted that "Hell's Kitchen is not a safe place for saved souls." Jesus' vision of holistic spirituality embraces every aspect of life, breaking down every dualism — body and spirit, individual and community, humanity and the non-human world — that negates human and non-human well-being. Indeed, our well-being may involve a combination of prayer and Prozac, and meditation and medication. It involves politics and economics as well.

Without going into detail about Jesus' healing methodology, we can make the following affirmations, grounded in the interplay of Jesus' healing ministry and progressive theology, essential for congregations seeking to be centers of holistic spirituality and healing:

- God seeks wholeness of body, mind, and spirit
- God desires that we have abundant life. Accordingly, God does not punish persons with disease or disaster, but seeks to deliver us from every form of heartbreak, alienation, and illness.
- Health and illness are the result from many factors, not just one. We cannot be fully responsible for our health or illness. Accidents as well as blessings occur in our lives.
- Body, mind, spirit, and relationships are intimately related.
- Healthy environments support personal well-being at every level.
- Economic justice and political access promote physical and spiritual well-being.
- God experiences our joy and pain, and as at work to bring us health and wholeness.
- Faith promotes greater personal well-being and opens the door for greater manifestations of God's love and energy.

– Wherever truth and healing are present, whether in science, meditation, spiritual practices, or scripture, God is its source.

The Church Ahead of us is a healing church. Every aspect of its mission is healing in nature, from planning worship to feeding persons experiencing poverty and homelessness. The church of the future responds to persons' desires for wholeness and provides a variety of entry points for joining faith and health. As a laboratory for healing and spirituality, the church will embrace global healing and spirituality in light of the healing gospel of Jesus Christ. Critically evaluating healing modalities and theologies and affirming maximal freedom and creativity, the church will join head, heart, and hands. With all their questions, seekers will be welcomed. While we may not have all the answers, theologically or scientifically speaking, we will be a place where everyone can find a home, regardless of their questions and doubts. Persons with illness of body, mind, and spirit will be welcomed and not blamed. In our prayers, we will anticipate the flow of God's healing energy to transform cells, souls, and communities. We will embody Jesus' healing touch in our prayers and practices and will be a place in which people find hope when a cure is no longer possible.

SPIRITUALITY AND ACTION FOR THE CHURCH AHEAD

Spiritual Adventures. Today, the church is challenged to be a laboratory for healing and wholeness. While healing does not involve violations of the laws of nature, our healing prayers and practices can open the door for an influx of healing energy that can change a person's life and promote greater physical, emotional, spiritual, and relational well-being. Our prayers and laying on of hands, whether in terms of liturgical laying on of hands, reiki healing touch, or other touch-oriented modalities, can transform cells as well as souls. Miracles can happen without supernatural interventions!

Our focus on healing invites you to make an experiment in prayerfulness. Make a commitment to be more focused in your prayer time. You can choose to pray for certain persons, speaking words of healing or visualizing them as whole. You can also reach out to them, inviting them to be part of a healing service at your church. Let your prayers transform your words and hands into instruments of healing.

Beyond that you can promote structures of healing in your community and nation in terms of health care accessibility, wellness care and preventative medicine, economic well-being, neighborhood safety, educational opportunity, and childcare. You can also explore how you and your church can support environmental health initiatives. As you consider the body politic in its brokenness, you can pray for the "opposition" but also seek healing encounters with those whose positions on the intersection of faith and politics radically differs from your own. Like Jesus, you can listen, seeking to understand the needs that underlie certain political positions. You can also examine your own bias and prejudice and repent of your own polarizing attitudes and activities. Much of the Western world, beginning with the USA, is on political life-support now: we need to move forward toward building bridges rather than walls and finding areas where we can join across faiths, theological positions, and politics in the healing of our land.

Contemplative Action. Many congregations are initiating health and healing ministries. Such ministries can have a variety of emphases ranging from visitation of shut-ins to healing clinics, complementary health practices, and companionship with the homeless. Your congregation might begin by asking questions such as: *What is our vision of healing? What role does prayer have in healing and wholeness? What are our attitudes toward complementary and global forms of healing? How do we feel about healing services? What type of healing service might best fit our congregation, given the spotlight given to dramatic healing services on television? Following your reflections, take one step to nurture the health and well-being of your congregation as you consider ways to reach out to the community.*

CHAPTER THIRTEEN

PROPHETIC HEALING

The spirit of the Lord GOD is upon me, because the LORD has anointed me; he has sent me to bring good news to the oppressed, to bind up the brokenhearted, to proclaim liberty to the captives, and release to the prisoners; to proclaim the year of the Lord's favor....to comfort all who mourn; to provide for those who mourn in Zion— to give them a garland instead of ashes, the oil of gladness instead of mourning, the mantle of praise instead of a faint spirit. They will be called oaks of righteousness, the planting of the LORD, to display his glory. (Isaiah 61:1-3)

The centrality of Jesus' and his spiritual predecessors' prophetic ministry as inspirations for responding to this present political darkness challenges me, as in the chapter on healing, to elaborate on points I introduced in Chapter Nine. The simple words "in the year Uzziah died" provide the backdrop for one of the most graphically described mystical experiences in scripture. Isaiah entered the Jerusalem Temple and to his amazement had a spiritual encounter with the God of Abraham, Isaac, and Jacob. Isaiah's world is turned upside down as he experiences the grandeur of God, receives God's healing touch, and then is presented with a question, "Whom will we send?" to which the prophet responds, "Send me." God sends Isaiah to speak the divine word to a nation in crisis. In a time of national instability, Isaiah presents God's vision of an alternative reality. Isaiah is called because God needs him. Justice and wholeness cannot be restored without human partnership.

As I write this text, the USA, Great Britain, and much of the Western world is in upheaval. The political and cultural center has collapsed. National consensus has dissolved. Families and friends have split over political differences. In the USA, the party in power and its president seem hell-bent on destroying the health care safety net, environmental protection, public education, anti-poverty programs, and support for the arts. Immigrants and citizens of color are frightened and Muslim citizens feel at risk for violence and governmental persecution. Hate crimes are on the upswing as evident in attacks on mosques and Jewish houses of worship. The dog whistles of racism are being blown each day as patriotism is being defined by the "great" days of white privilege rather than liberty and justice for all. Saber-rattling has become the norm in foreign policy as leaders treat nuclear weapons as if they are schoolyard toys. The middle class is shrinking as tax policy threatens to expand the gap between the richest Americans and average wage earners and the working poor. An abundant nation, with great power, we are living by scarcity and fear. The global pandemic has pushed us further into our political, economic, and international siloes.

Within the halls of Congress focus on profits has drowned out the message of the prophets as public policy privileges the wealthy over the vulnerable. Our leaders have given up any pretense of providing moral leadership here and abroad. Sadly, some of the most ardent champions of policies that lead to environmental destruction, economic inequality, and financial privilege are church members, whose loyalties seem to be more aligned with small government and corporate profit than care for the vulnerable and marginalized. Only a transformed spirit, embodied in innovative partnerships, can move our communities and nation forward.

Prophetic Visioning

The times cry out for a prophetic vision. In a time of crisis, the church is challenged to be a headlight and not a tail light, as Martin Luther King asserted. The nation is need of prophetic healing, grounded in the difficult — and almost impossible — blending of pastoral care and prophetic possibility. In contrast to Hebraic and contemporary prophets whose vocations were freestanding and had no institutional loyalties, the prophetic mission of congregations and their leaders is especially difficult since congregational callings involve integrating the care and critique of communities with ongoing institutional histories and politically diverse memberships. As a congregational pastor, I am called to speak a prophetic word to a unique community in a manner that includes political diversity rather than excludes those whose positions are different than my own theological and ethical viewpoint. The temptation is to do nothing, but in doing nothing, or in preaching feel-good messages that don't address the pain millions experience, we will become complicit in the destruction of our nation and the planet.

The prophetic word is grounded in vision, interdependence, and divine-human partnership. As Walter Brueggemann rightly notes, the prophet's calling is to present an alternative vision to the current social injustice. Since virtually every political and economic system neglects some of its members, the prophetic critique is always in season, challenging both the left and the right for its sins of omission and commission. Prophets remind us that our world can be different than it is. Justice can roll down like waters and righteousness like an ever-flowing stream. National and corporate leaders can do justice, love mercy, and walk humbly with God. Worship can be joined with social justice and prayer with protest. From the perspective of God's vision of Shalom, the peaceable realm toward which the moral arc of history leans, all systems fall short and need the inspiration of an alternative vision.

Prophets are apostles of interdependence. Wealth and poverty are interconnected. White privilege, racism, and African American poverty are intimately related. Earth, air, sky, and sea exist in a dynamic synergy with neighborhoods and industrial parks. This profound interdependence even includes God, as Rabbi Abraham Heschel noted in his description of the "divine pathos." What happens on earth matters in heaven. God grieves over the cries of the poor. God is angered by the growing gap between the poor and wealthy. God challenges tax policies and governmental programs that take food from the hungry, condemn single mothers to poverty, build pipelines over sacred grounds, and reduce tax rates for wealthy individuals and corporations while reducing expenditures on environmental protection and food stamps. God hears the cries of the poor. God feels the pain of the marginalized. God experiences the defensiveness of those who have experienced the privileges of race, economics and education. God is with us in our suffering and enjoyment and is the fellow sufferer who not only understands but convicts and challenges. Biblical spirituality invites us not only to side with God's vision of Shalom but also listen prayerfully for God's pain in the cries of the poor and to experience that pain as well. God's vision transcends partisan politics and challenges us to live by the values of heaven in our day to day personal and corporate responsibilities.

Pastor as Prophet and Prophet as Pastor

Many pastors struggle to find their prophetic voice. But, find it we must. We must awaken ourselves to the cries of the poor in our neighborhood. While we don't need to be partisan, we are challenged to sensitize ourselves and our congregations to the realities of pain and neglect in our communities. In the spirit of anti-war activist Father Daniel Berrigan, we can speak truth to power noting that our task is to affirm that God's justice should flow like waters while the task of government is to build effective irrigation ditches.

The business of the church is healing in its many dimensions, both personal and corporate. Our calling is to respond to anything that stands in the way of God's vision of abundant life. For some pastors and congregations, this involves direct social involvement to improve the life of vulnerable people — soup kitchens, casseroles for homeless shelters, support of parents of persons with substance abuse issues, mentoring and tutoring of at-risk children, and involvement in local environmental issues. Other congregations are called to "picket and pray" with the New Poor Peoples March or in their local community, unsafe nuclear power plants, and the offices of political officials advocating policies that privilege the wealthy or unfairly respond to immigrants and refugees. We can affirm the value of both women and fetuses, and provide for contraception, as we seek a way beyond the impasse of abortion. Recognizing the destructive impact of poverty on children and families, we can, across party lines and political and theological viewpoints, remember the fiftieth anniversary of the Poor Peoples March in 2018 and make it a yearly event, and seek justice and peace in season and out.

There are many models of prophetic ministry, and today's pastors must balance in politically diverse communities, pastoral care with prophetic concern. Settled pastors need to focus on values that transcend partisanship and that unity rather than polarize congregations. It is easy for us to demonize our political opponents and their allies. We need to see Christ in those politicians who foment chaos and polarization and pray that they — and every citizen, including ourselves — respond to the better angels of our natures. We need to create sanctuaries for safe conversation as well as healing action, where prophetic action joins rather than destroys our congregational life.

As Brian McLaren asserts, the planet is on fire. We can no longer sit on the sidelines. We must confess, in the spirit of Thomas Merton, that we are all guilty bystanders. While we may not be able relinquish our racial or economic privilege, we can become people whose calling is to heal the planet and its people. In our interdependent universe, God needs us and congregations that join compassion with prophetic challenge. God is all-loving, but not all-determining. God's vision of Shalom needs our commitment and partnership as we embrace our vocation to be God's partners in healing the Earth. God needs our help — and right now — to heal the world one act and one phone call at a time.

Spirituality and Action for the Church Ahead

Spiritual Adventures. Scripture is intended to be a book of living prayer. Set aside a portion of daily over a week's period to immerse yourself in the Book of Amos. Listen for God's voice in the prophet's denunciation of economic inequality and injustice. Attend to the complacency of the wealthy and powerful and consider your own complacency and complicity in promoting, however unintentionally and indirectly, death and injustice among the marginalized and vulnerable. Imagine how you and your congregation might avoid a "famine of hearing God's word."

As you reflect prayerfully on your own congregation's call to prophetic healing, take time to reflect on Amos' challenging questions:

- Where is economic inequality in your community?
- What are the hidden faces of poverty?
- Where is their human trafficking (modern-day slavery) in your community?
- Where do you see corporate dishonesty?
- What aren't we seeing in our neighborhood? What types of suffering are we choosing to avoid? Where are our spirits deadened by apathy|?
- What is your — and your leaders' — vested interest in maintaining the unjust status quo?
- How is your wealth, for example, the growth of your retirement plan or stock values related to destruction of the Earth?
- Knowing that we will always be complicit with injustice as a result of our privilege, how can you minimize your role in destroying the Earth and its most vulnerable people?
- How can you find common ground with persons of different theological and political perspectives?

Ask God to give you and your congregation a vision, or guidance, to respond with mercy and kindness, and ways to let justice flow down like waters in your own interactions and political involvement.

Contemplative Actions. Our reflections call us to action to heal the earth and its peoples. This vision may be translated into "better angels" (in the spirit of Abraham Lincoln's counsel) or "sacred conversation" groups that address central political and social issues across party and ideological lines.

These prophetic healing groups can be surrounded by prayer and constructed as safe places for honest dialogue between persons with contrasting positions. These groups can also have an underlying goal of seeking ways to move forward together where we are able, placing our disagreements on hold or in the background to focus on matters of life and death in our communities. Motivated by Jesus' affirmation that how we respond to the "least of these" touches the heart of God, we may be able to transcend differing positions in our quest to be God's companions in healing the earth. We may also choose to become active in challenging our political leaders to embody compassion and care for the vulnerable in their political decisions as well as responding to the hungry, homeless and marginalized in our community.

Chapter Fourteen

All Who Wander Are Not Lost

J.R.R. Tolkien notes that "not all those who wander are lost." This statement could easily describe the postmodern, progressive and emerging Christian movement. We are constantly having to rewrite our spiritual and congregational maps. Like the emerging first-century Christian movement, we choose to take certain paths and not others. Some paths lead to dead ends. Other paths cut off lively possibilities. Fearful of alternative paths, some seek denominational and theological certainty in adhering to authoritative scriptures, church structures, and theologies, but such clarity is often bought at the price of stifling further revelations of God's Spirit.

Like the first Christians described in Acts of the Apostles, we must awaken to God's presence through prayer and communal wisdom to give us enough direction for the next steps in our spiritual journeys. Like the earliest followers of Jesus, we find ourselves often making it up as we go along, threading the needle between tradition and novelty. Honoring the past yet choosing not to be mired in approaches that no longer work. Embracing the future yet recognizing that novelty for its own sake leaves us directionless and subject to the latest cultural or spiritual trends.

While cannot predict our destination, we must move forward in faith. An ancient saying proclaims, *Solvitur ambulando,* "it is solved in the walking." Like Jesus and the women and men who followed him, we must be a peripatetic church. We must awaken to divine possibilities, trusting God's lure for adventure. The spirituality of the future must be adventurous because God is adventurous. God is faithful through all life's seasons, but God's mercies are new every morning. There are no simple or easy answers, nor are there surefire "how-to" instruction books, for the future of postmodern, progressive and emerging Christianity. There is, however, trust that God is with us, that God is constantly inspiring us, and that when we listen to God's wisdom, we will find our way. We need, as the author of Psalm 46 counsels, to be still and know that God is with us.

We need to remember the experience of young Howard Thurman, when he was caught in a thunderstorm, as we face the threatening storms of our time. Out on a berry picking expedition, young Howard Thurman found himself lost in the woods as a storm was descending. Startled by a flash of lightning, Thurman found himself in an unfamiliar environment. Tempted to panic, and simply run in whatever direction lay ahead him, Thurman remembered the wisdom of his elders, "When you don't know where you are, stop and wait until you find your bearings." He stopped. Lightning flashed and he looked ahead. Another stroke of lightning and he looked to the left. With another he looked behind. He kept looking until he saw something familiar. Step by step, he found his way home, guided by his inner wisdom and the storm that enveloped him.

God is in the storm with us just as God was present with Jesus' followers in the storm at sea. God is in the social upheaval and the spiritual maelstrom that surrounds us. To our surprise and chagrin, there are times when God is the storm-giver, calling us from complacency to commitment. Still, God's quiet — and sometimes lively — providence is with us as we step forward not expecting to see the far horizon; but finding our way one step at a time. One step, one act, and then the next one and another, is enough as we imagine the Church Ahead.

ALSO FROM ENERGION PUBLICATIONS
Guides to Practical Ministry

In this clear, concise and hope-filled book Ruth Fletcher offers substantive help and direction to congregational leaders and pastors alike. Grounded in her years of experience in a wide variety of church settings, her faithful observation of human life and her deep love of God, Ruth tells us stories of transformation that arise like green shoots from the most unexpected and unlikely of places.

Rev. Laurie Rudel
Pastor, Queen Anne
Christian Church
Seattle, Washington

FROM ANOTHER
ACADEMY OF PARISH CLERGY AUTHOR

Bob Cornwall provides a vision for today's Christians, centered around living out our gifts in creative and life-transforming ways. We are gifted, even when we are unaware of it.
Bruce Epperly, PhD
Pastor and Author

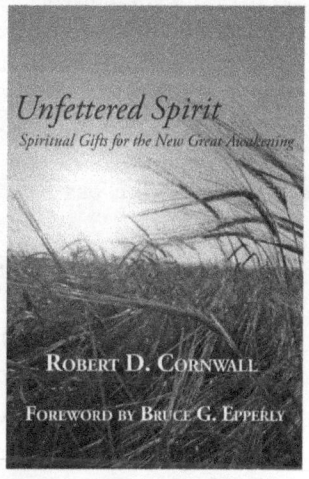

MORE FROM ENERGION PUBLICATIONS

ACADEMY OF PARISH CLERGY SERIES AND AUTHORS

Conversations in Ministry

Clergy Table Talk	Kent Ira Groff	$9.99
Out of the Office	Robert D. Cornwall	$9.99
Wind and Whirlwind	David Moffett-Moore	$9.99

Guides to Practical Ministry

Overcoming Sermon Block	William Powell Tuck	$12.99
Thrive	Ruth Fletcher	$14.99
In Changing Times	Ron Higdon	$14.99

Academy Member Authors (Selected Titles)

Faith in the Public Square	Robert D. Cornwall	$16.99
Ephesians: A Participatory Study Guide		$9.99
Ultimate Allegiance		$9.99
The Authority of Scripture in a Postmodern Age		$5.99
From Words of Woe to Unbelievable News		$5.99
The Eucharist		$5.99
Unfettered Spirit		$14.99
From Here to Eternity	Bruce Epperly	$5.99
Angels, Mysteries, and Miracles		$9.99
Transforming Acts		$14.99
Jonah: When God Changes		$5.99
Process Theology: Embracing Adventure with God		$5.99
The Journey to the Undiscovered Country	William Powell Tuck	$9.99
Creation in Contemporary Experience	David Moffett-Moore	$9.99
Life as Pilgrimage		$14.99
The Spirit's Fruit		$9.99
The Jesus Manifesto		$9.99
Spiritual Care Reflections	Charles J. Lopez, Jr.	$14.99

Generous Quantity Discounts Available
Dealer Inquiries Welcome
Energion Publications — P.O. Box 841
Gonzalez, FL_ 32560
Website: http://energionpubs.com
Phone: (850) 525-3916

www.ingramcontent.com/pod-product-compliance
Lightning Source LLC
LaVergne TN
LVHW041629070426
835507LV00008B/526